D1156493

Studies in modern capitalism · Etudes sur le capitalisme moderne

Mexican agriculture 1521–1630

Studies in modern capitalism · Etudes sur le capitalisme moderne

Editorial board · Comité de rédaction
Maurice Aymard, Maison des Sciences de l'Homme, Paris
Jacques Revel, Ecole des Hautes Etudes en Sciences Sociales, Paris
Immanuel Wallerstein, Fernand Braudel Center for the Study of Economies, Historical Systems, and Civilizations, Binghamton, New York

This series is devoted to an attempt to comprehend capitalism as a world-system. It will include monographs, collections of essays and colloquia around specific themes, written by historians and social scientists united by a common concern for the study of large-scale long-term social structure and social change.

The series is a joint enterprise of the Maison des Sciences de l'Homme in Paris and the Fernand Braudel Center for the Study of Economies, Historical Systems, and Civilizations at the State University of New York at Binghamton.

Other books in the series

Immanuel Wallerstein: *The capitalist world-economy*
Pierre Bourdieu: *Algeria 1960*

This book is published as part of the joint publishing agreement established in 1977 between the Fondation de la Maison des Sciences de l'Homme and the Syndics of the Cambridge University Press. Titles published under this arrangement may appear in any European language or, in the case of volumes of collected essays, in several languages.

New books will appear either as individual titles or in one of the series which the Maison des Sciences de l'Homme and the Cambridge University Press have jointly agreed to publish. All books published jointly by the Maison des Sciences de l'Homme and the Cambridge University Press will be distributed by the Press throughout the world.

Mexican agriculture 1521–1630

Transformation of the mode of production

ANDRE GUNDER FRANK

Cambridge University Press

Cambridge London New York Melbourne

& Editions de la Maison des Sciences de l'Homme

Paris

607439

Published by the Syndics of the Cambridge University Press
The Pitt Building, Trumpington Street, Cambridge CB2 1RP
Bentley House, 200 Euston Road, London NW1 2DB
32 East 57th Street, New York, NY 10022, USA
296 Beaconsfield Parade, Middle Park, Melbourne 3206, Australia
and Editions de la Maison des Sciences de l'Homme
54 Boulevard Raspail, 75270 Paris Cedex 06

© Andre Gunder Frank 1979

First Published 1979

Printed in Great Britain at the
University Press, Cambridge

Library of Congress Cataloguing in Publication Data
Frank, Andre Gunder, 1929–
Mexican agriculture, 1521–1630.
(Studies in modern capitalism)
Bibliography: p.
Includes index.
1. Agriculture – Economic aspects – Mexico –
History. 2. Mexico – Rural conditions. I. Title.
II. Series.
HD1792.F7   1979   338.1'0972   78-6201
ISBN 0 521 22209 5

Contents

Preface

The research reflected in the following pages was undertaken in 1965, while I was Professor at the National School of Economics at the National Autonomous University of Mexico and Research Associate in its Institute of Economic Research. It was written up in 1966 when I was serving as Professor in the Departments of Economics and History at Sir George Williams University in Montreal, Canada. Apart from a few minor changes, including the addition of a list of references, the manuscript has remained unrevised, and is published as such due to the following circumstances and reasons.

At the time the research was undertaken, a simple collection and ordering of the most salient facts seemed to be a useful task in the absence of any single history of Mexican agriculture. What is more, it seemed important to confront the theoretical and ideological challenges of a time in which the thesis of 'feudalism', especially in agriculture, was still dominant in Latin America (and its political implications were widespread, see Frank 1967 and Frank 1969). The standard historical works on agriculture in Mexico, like those of Jesús Silva Herzog, dealt with 'agrarianismo' or agricultural policy, and did not offer an analysis of the history of agrarian reality. The only study available on this topic was the *Economía y política en la historia de México* by Manuel López Gallo, which had just been published and was soon reprinted, and was in all respects unsatisfactory. At the same time there appeared the politically important *Democracia en México* by Pablo González Casanova which, apart from other objectionable features (see Frank 1969: chapter 20), used a faulty analysis of Mexico's past as its 'scientific' basis.

My own study of Mexican agriculture was intended to help fill this then existing scientific void and thereby to intervene in the political debate of the time. (Since then vast scientific advances have been made by others and the terms of the political debate have changed as well.)

The review, analysis and interpretation of the transformation and development of the modes of agricultural production in Mexico during the first century after the Spanish conquest, which is now published here, was originally intended as the first part of a study entitled 'Mexican agriculture from conquest to Revolution: an economic historical interpretation'. The following extract from the original description of this research project (dated 16 December 1965) will give an idea of the scope of the project as a whole, of the context in which this text should be seen, and of the hypothesis on which the work is based.

I propose to collect and analyse data about the state and development of Mexican agriculture over four centuries from the conquest to 1910, and I hope to contribute to the greater clarification of these fundamental problems: the transformation brought about by conquest and colonization in the sixteenth century and then again during the 'seventeenth century of depression'; the causes of the development of the *hacienda* and its economic function; the agricultural background of Independence; the causes and consequences of the *manos muertos* of Church property; the economic currents that led to the Reform and the economic interests at stake; the relations between agriculture and the Porfirian Peace; the nature of the Mexican Revolution; and certain analogies between the causes and consequences of Independence, Reform and Revolution as well as agrarian reform, and between these and similar events in other parts of Latin America.

I hope to achieve the following goals: first, to assemble data about four centuries of agricultural reality, rather than (the more usually discussed) 'agrarianism' or agrarian policy and reform. This work should facilitate access of other researchers to such data which are still widely dispersed among many sources. Second, I hope to find and expose the thread of historical development which passes through these realities of Mexican agriculture and which relates them to world and national development. Thereby, I also hope to contribute to the study and understanding of Mexican and Latin American past and present in general.

Finally, I hope to test the facts and offer a different interpretation of some widely accepted theses, for example:

(1) The thesis of Chevalier and Borah that the Mexican *hacienda* 'consolidated' itself in the 'century of depression' in which agriculture 'involuted' is, I suggest, disproved by their own and other researchers' data. I propose to test the opposite hypothesis that 'the formation of the great latifundium in Mexico' (as well as in other Latin American countries) was due to an

increase in the market demand and price for its products, not only in the sixteenth and seventeenth centuries (mining and urban demand), but also in the eighteenth century (mining and free trade demand), in the nineteenth century (economic development), and again in the twentieth century (foreign and industrial demand).

(2) The thesis of subsistence agriculture in a closed economy can be confronted by facts that suggest a little appreciated but very appreciable level of commercialization of agriculture, of the farmer, and of the (indigenous) peasant, all of which seem to respond to and adapt themselves to economic cycles of regional, national and international demand and supply throughout Mexican history. I wish to show that it is this base of economic change and development, more than the so-called archaic institutions and the legislative reforms, that constitutes the principal determinant of the economic and cultural wealth and poverty of the Mexican people. At the same time, I wish to test against the historical facts the doubtful thesis that an increase in demand and development necessarily brings with it a general increase in wealth and welfare, and the contrary hypothesis that very often demand and development generate a greater degree of misery for a large part of the peasant class.

(3) The thesis that the land in New Spain belonged to and suffered because of the *manos muertos* of the Church does not stand up to historical evidence. The Church was in possession of the land from the time of Independence. I propose to locate and explain this occurrence within the agricultural and economic decline of the times and to analyse its economic significance.

(4) It is customary to interpret the Reform in terms of liberalism and individualism, but I propose to examine it within its economic context and with reference to the improvement and increase of agricultural business as part of the general economic upswing. These were, I suggest, more the cause of this Reform than its consequence. I suggest that reform appeared in various Latin American countries at different times because the necessary economic circumstances appeared at different times. [This hypothesis has since been partially examined and confirmed in Frank 1972: chapter 5.] Examination of the circumstances surrounding the Reform will permit a better appreciation of its economic and social consequences.

(5) I propose to examine these and other problems with the most readily available historical material from the Porfiriato, in which many old problems reappear in a new context, which renders them sufficiently acute to lead to the Revolution.

I hope that this study will lead to the concrete support of my hypotheses, and that an interpretation of the Independence, Reform, Revolution and agrarian reform will emerge out of the study of the economic reality of the social system and the historical development which produced these major national movements in Mexico, and others elsewhere in Latin America. Perhaps the study will thus contribute to the better comprehension of the successes that these social movements had or failed to have in Mexico and to a better appreciation of the success that analogous movements could have elsewhere in Latin America.

Finally and most importantly, I hope that the assembly of these data and the proposition of these and other hypotheses will help and encourage other researchers who are better able to pursue the directions outlined here.

Other responsibilities and undertakings unfortunately pre-
vented me from pursuing and completing this study of Mexican
agriculture from conquest to Revolution as intended. I was able
to prepare a written text of my analysis of only the first century
after the conquest, and it is this text which is now published
as the present book. My never written analysis of the historical
evidence for later periods does, however, support the foregoing
hypotheses as follows. The first attempt at Mexican independence under the leadership of Hidalgo and Morelos was in part
a response to the increased exploitation of labour which
resulted from the accelerated growth of agricultural and mining
production (stimulated by the increase and liberalization of
foreign trade at the end of the eighteenth century). The
greater weight of *manos muertos* and the lower efficiency of land
use after Independence were due primarily to the general
economic and agricultural 'depression' of the time. The liberal
reform of the mid nineteenth century was caused by economic
revival, which it then promoted further. The organization and
development of agricultural production during the Porfiriato
obeyed challenges and opportunities generated by imperialism
(and not inherited from feudalism), causing a crisis so acute
as to produce the Mexican Revolution of 1910, which was
sparked off by the American recession of 1907.

Beyond the projected study of agriculture in Mexico, I had
intended to apply the economic analysis implicit in the above
hypotheses to the comparative study of the growth and development of the latifundium elsewhere in Latin America.
Accordingly, my research seminar in the sociology department
of the Universidad de Chile began the analysis, comparison
and interpretation of the growth and development of the
latifundium in eighteenth- and nineteenth-century Chile, in
nineteenth-century Argentina, Cuba and São Paulo, and in
other areas insofar as the available literature permitted. The
intention was to use these studies to analyse varieties, appear-
ance and *essence* of organizational forms, mode of production
and their transformation in contemporary agriculture in Chile
and Mexico. Some preliminary aspects of the line of study are
published in Frank 1972: chapters 2 and 5 (on agrarian structure
and liberal reforms respectively).

The study of Mexican agriculture now published here is limited to a much shorter historical period and a narrower topical range than the study outlined above. Nonetheless, the analysis in the text as published here is strongly influenced – indeed substantially determined – by the theoretical scope of the unfinished larger study. At the same time, I hope that the theoretical scope of this short text may still prove useful – if not determinant – for the analysis of the longer period and wider range of problems posed by Mexican and Latin American agricultural development to our day. On the other hand, the recent very substantial advance of work on Mexican agricultural history by other researchers has advanced far beyond my own capacities. Therefore, my own continuation of this study would now be out of place; and even the revision of the present manuscript to take account of these advances would be out of the question. Moreover, under present circumstances the study of urban, industrial and international political economic forces and developments on a world scale assume greater urgency and importance for me than further research into Mexican agrarian problems.

Therefore, I face the alternatives of leaving my existing manuscript to rest forever in my files or of publishing it as it is. Three main considerations induce me to now publish my text as this book. Firstly, its use and citation by Alonso Aguilar in his *Dialéctica de la economía mexicana* suggests that some other students of these and related problems may still derive some benefit from the work that went into the preparation of this manuscript. Secondly, there is a renewed interest in the history of colonial times and in the analysis or reinterpretation of modes of production then and since then. This interest is reflected in the success of books like Stanley and Barbara Stein's *Colonial Heritage of Latin America*; in the publication of historical studies of Mexico and elsewhere in the Latin American Series by Cambridge University Press; in the excellent new economic historical research by many Mexican authors, including especially Enrique Florescano and other historians at the Colegio de México; and in general the lively debate on the reinterpretation of dependence through the analysis of modes of production in Latin America and other parts of the world, which rages through the journals there and elsewhere. All this literature is becoming so abundant as to render its citation here impossible. In this context, the present book may constitute an additional grain of sand. Thirdly, in much of this literature, I am criticized for having devoted excessive attention in my publications to the relations of exchange and thereby supposedly excluding the relations of production. Without wishing to accept or answer these charges here, I would like to make available to my critics and other readers an analysis of some aspects of agriculture which, though written long ago, perhaps dedicates relatively more attention to the relations of production, and which tries to account for and explain them, though possibly still not to the satisfaction of my critics and certainly not to my own.

Santiago de Chile, 1972   A.G.F.
Frankfurt, 1978

Acknowledgements and dedication

I wish to extend my thanks to many friends and institutions for the help and support which made it possible for this work finally to see the light of day more than a decade after its preparation: to the National School of Economics (then under the direction of Horacio Flores de la Peña) and the Institute of Economics Research (whose Director at the time was José Luis Ceceña) at the National Autonomous University of Mexico (UNAM), and especially the *compañeros* Alonso Aguilar, Arturo Bonilla and Fernando Carmona for their support while I was doing the research on Mexican agriculture which underlies this essay (as well as that on later periods which I was never able to write up); to the Louis M. Rabinowitz Foundation of New York for financial support at that time; to the secretaries at the Department of Economics of Sir George Williams University in Montreal, Canada, who in 1966 took great care in transcribing many tapes dictated with strange words and names; to my wife, Marta Fuentes, for her unlimited moral support in the preparation of this work and in the decision to publish it, as well as for her help in revising the manuscript and in preparing the list of references (not all of which we were able to locate again after so many years and without my personal library); to Margaret Fay and Susan Jupp and the staff of Cambridge University Press for editing the manuscript; to the Max Planck Institute in Starnberg, Germany and the German Foundation for Peace and Conflict Research (DGFK) for the opportunity to edit and reproduce the manuscript; and to Immanuel Wallerstein and the Fernand Braudel Center, to Clemens Heller and Maurice Aymard at the Maison des Sciences de l'Homme and

Jacques Revel for their decision to publish this essay in the series Studies in Modern Capitalism. At the same time, I should like to take this opportunity also to thank here the *compañeros* of the Publications Committee of the Student Center of the National School of Anthropology and History in Mexico who have translated this essay into Spanish and have undertaken to publish it in that language.

I should like to dedicate this modest essay and the incomplete work that it represents to 'committed' anthropological and historical research and especially to its committed *compañeros* in Mexico – committed to their people, to their culture and to their un-institutionalized revolution – whose own revolutionary dedication and responsible criticism of institutional *indigenismo* and other forms of populism do not deserve the unjust treatment to which they are sometimes subjected.

Munich, 1975   A.G.F.
Frankfurt, 1978

Part I

The impossibility of the dual economy

1 ❧ Introduction: the economic genesis of social institutions

We begin our inquiry into the economic history of Mexican agriculture during the century after the Spanish conquest by posing the question which will be central to our inquiry throughout: how is the organization of agricultural production and distribution determined? Whether there is meat in the kitchen is never determined in the kitchen. It depends on the household and on the total economy. Similarly, the most important events and most fundamental institutions in the history of Mexican agriculture cannot simply be explained as the result of the exercise of conscious intent by particular individuals either within or outside Mexican agriculture. We will see that the economic organization and social institutions of agriculture in Mexico have, throughout its history, grown out of the developmental needs and capacities of an economic system of which Mexican agriculture formed only a part. This system was mercantile capitalism, a system which soon after the Spanish conquest of Mexico was to embrace the entire world.

Christopher Columbus, the discoverer of America, had declared: 'The best thing in the world is gold... It can even send souls to heaven.' Cortés, the conqueror of Mexico, added: 'The Spaniards are troubled with a disease of the heart for which gold is the specific remedy.' The Franciscan friars confirmed:

1

'There is no place for religion without silver.' Neither the conquerors nor the colonizers came to Mexico in search of food. They came in search of gold and silver and of the Indian labour needed to extract this wealth. To the colonists the Mexican land and its fruits were no more than the necessary inputs to sustain this productive process. The production of precious metals required food, shelter and clothing for the workers and the colonists, as well as tools and materials for the extraction and transport of the metals. Thus, after the Spanish conquest, the utility and profitability of Mexican agriculture resulted in its becoming a by-product of the colonial economy and its development, just as the colonial economy itself was a by-product of – and contributed to – the world-wide expansion and development of the mercantile capitalist system.

Sergio Bagú has characterized this system and Latin America's place in it thus:

By multiplying mercantile capital and stimulating international trade, the commercial revolution, which had begun in the fifteenth century, linked the fate of one nation or another, intensifying economic interdependence. The type of economy which the Iberian metropolis organized was of a definite colonial nature, oriented to the Central and West European markets. The same purpose motivated the Portuguese–Spanish producers in the new continent. Colonial capitalism, rather than feudalism, was the type of economic structure which appeared in America in the period we are studying. . . Iberian America was born to integrate the cycle of incipient capitalism, not to prolong the languishing feudal cycle. . . If there is a well-defined and unquestionable feature of the colonial economy, it is production for the market. From the first to the last days of the colonial regime, this characteristic conditions all productive enterprise. . . This is how the trends which then predominated in European international markets formed the principal elements shaping the colonial economic structure. It might be added that this phenomenon is characteristic of all colonial economies whose subordination of foreign markets has been, and still is, the principal cause of deformation and lethargy.   (Bagu 1949: 39, 68, 117, 260)

The place of Mexico or New Spain in the mercantile capitalist system has been analysed by Eduardo Arcila Farías:

The Spanish empire had two centres in America through which it maintained its cohesion and its unity. These two centres were Mexico and Peru. . . The economic influence of New Spain extended over a large part of Spanish territory in America and created a close dependence that tied to it a great number of these provinces, who looked towards New Spain as the real metropolis. In this way, one might say that a large number of the Spanish dominions in America were dominions more of Mexico than of Spain, if we consider the direct relations and economic ties between them. . . It is possible, then, to speak of a Mexican colonial empire in America.

(Arcila Farías 1950: 19)

This empire comprised the entire circum-Caribbean region of North and South America and the islands in between.

Mexico itself has been aptly characterized by Eric Wolf:

The Indian before the conquest had been a cultivator, a seed-planter. The conquering Spaniard became a mining entrepreneur, a producer of commercial crops, a rancher, a merchant. The strategic economic relationship of the pre-Conquest period united Indian peasant and Indian lord, tribute-producer and tribute-consumer. The goal of the Indian noble was to consume wealth commensurate with his social position. The Spanish colonist, however, labored for different ends. He wanted to convert wealth and labor into salable goods – into gold and silver, hides and wool, wheat and sugar cane. . . The motor of this capitalism was mining. (Wolf 1959: 176)

The new institutions that grew up were far more an outgrowth of past development and a response to the exigencies of contemporary times than a determinant of future development. José Ots Capdequí writes:

It is not impossible to penetrate into the heart of the real historical significance of the social, economic, and legal institutions incorporated into the so-called Indian law [*derecho indiano*], which refers not to Indians but to the Indies as Spanish America was then called. If one does not keep in mind this historical fact which I have amply dealt with in some of my writings: that the task of the discovery, conquest, and colonization of America was not in the strict sense, in its origins, a state enterprise. . . if we analyse the whole of the *capitulaciones* (grants) that are preserved in the general archives of the Indies of Seville we find clear evidence of the absorbing predominance of private interests, and of private initiative in the organization and the maintenance of the exploratory expedition. It was normal for these expeditions to be financed by great merchants. . . Under the new law that arose in the eastern countries, the strictly Indian [American] rights had a fundamentally contractual character. . . these *capitulaciones*, these contracts, became truly juridical and negotiable instruments; and before the business venture based on them was undertaken, they were subject to exchange, transfer, purchase, and sale, corporate contract. (Ots Capdequí 1946: 8–11)

When the Spanish conquerors arrived, they found an Indian population estimated at 11 to 25 million people living in central Mexico. The estimate of 11 million was published by Cook and Simpson in 1948 and is cited by Borah (1951: 3). The estimate of 25 million was published by Borah and Cook (1962: 5). The population of the Valley of Mexico alone has been estimated at 1,500,000 (Gibson 1964: 6). This immense, highly civilized population was the principal resource available to the Spaniards for mining, a resource more important than Mexico's mines and far more important than its land. For as Eric Wolf has said, 'All the claims to utopia – economic, religious, and political – rested ultimately upon the management and control of but one resource: the indigenous population of the colony. The conquerors wanted Indian labor, the crown Indian subjects, the friars Indian souls' (Wolf 1959: 195). The Spaniards, of course, did not come to kill the goose that laid the golden egg. But they did, through exploitation and disease. Little more than a century later only a million to a million and a half Indians were left (Borah 1951: 3 and Borah and Cook 1962: 5). Though Borah and Cook contend that Mexico was condemned to suffer a population disaster even without the conquest, the enormity of the disaster that in fact took place can be attributed to Spanish conquest and colonization (Borah and Cook 1962: 7). Inevitably, this momentous and rapid decline of the Indian population and labour force, in the face of a growing demand for the fruits of its labour by the white population on both sides of the Atlantic, was to play a key part in shaping Mexico's rural institutions, in determining its history in general and its agricultural history in particular.

The Spanish intent, apparently, was to graft their own economy on to the existing indigenous one and merely to skim the cream off the top of the latter for the benefit of the former. Gibson suggests that 'It was not the intention of Spaniards to interfere in the more prosaic aspects of native commodity production... The earliest conception was of a separation of trade' between the Spanish and Indian economies (Gibson 1964: 335, 360). Indeed, referring to the Indian economy, Gibson maintains that 'no immediate or drastic transformation occurred in native markets with the establishment of the Spanish colony' (Gibson 1964: 353–3). And Mendizábal elaborates:

As far as its lowest strata were concerned, neither the forms of economic production nor those of social organization of the vanquished were modified immediately. The surplus value was simply drained off in favour of the new privileged classes: kings, conquerors, friars, merchants and administrators. Agricultural production, with the exception of the new crops – wheat, olives, grapes etc. – was directed by the Spanish conquerors or colonists but worked by native labour, the industries . . . everything that was economically productive work remained for many years allotted to the Indians with the help, which was of little importance, of a few thousand African Negro slaves.

(Mendizábal 1945–6: IV, 59).

Like the Moguls and other conquerors of the peasants on the Indian sub-continent or like the Aztecs and previous conquerors of the peasants in middle America, many conquerors throughout history had endeavoured to skim tribute off the top of the conquered economy, while leaving the economic and social organization of the conquered peoples as undisturbed as possible, so that it might produce a maximum of surplus for both conqueror and conquered alike at minimum cost to the former. Previous conquerors had in many cases not only tried but succeeded (see Marx on India, Lattimore on China, Wolf on Mexico). But as we shall see, in the case of the Spanish conquest of America and of New Spain this policy did not succeed. Only a very few years after the conquest, it proved to be impossible to maintain the separation of the colonial Spanish and Indian economies or to invoke the Spanish conquerors' protection, *noblesse oblige*, of the crown's new Indian subjects. Despite the measures that the Spanish colonizers took to protect their Indian subjects and the Indian economy from disturbance, Indian life and Mexican agriculture were increasingly integrated – ironically through these very measures – into the mercantile capitalist system. The structure and development of this system demanded a type of colonization unlike any that history had previously known. As we shall see, the Spanish desire to preserve the Indian economy as a separate sector was thwarted not so much by commercialization *per se*, as by the commercial integration of the Mexican economy and its agriculture into the expanding world mercantile capitalist system. The participation of the Spanish colonists in this world system generated objective needs, the pursuit of which necessarily drew the entire Indian population and its economy into the system as well. It became increasingly impossible to leave the Indian economy and agriculture undisturbed and merely to scoop off tribute. Capitalist tribute differs from tributes in other modes of production in that its extraction and its use for the development of one part of the system necessarily generates the underdevelopment of another part of the system. The underdeveloped part of the mercantile capitalit system included most of Mexican agriculture.

Enrique Florescano's periodization of the history of Spanish grain legislation is highly significant to an understanding of the impact of Spanish colonization on Mexican agriculture. Florescano divides the Spanish grain legislation passed during the sixteenth century into three periods, each period having particular characteristics of its own. The importance of Spanish legislation, we should argue, was not that it determined historical developments but rather that it ratified or adjusted to an already changed reality. Florescano's periodization based on the changing characteristics of grain legislation serves as a rough basis for understanding critical changes in the reality of colonial grain production and hence for defining the sixteenth-century history of Mexican agriculture as a whole.

The first period, Florescano suggests, runs to 1550 and is characterized by the anarchic fumbling of the Spanish conquerors. The second period runs to 1579 and represents, he suggests, a more systematic effort to regulate grain supplies and prices. The third period, beginning in 1580 and for Florescano ending in 1595 – though in many respects it can be said to run on into the seventeenth century – is the period of the major Spanish effort to organize agricultural supplies to meet Spanish needs (Florescano 1965a: 604). Florescano himself notes elsewhere, as does Gibson, that the major legislation that initiated the second and third periods was definitely prompted by the historical events which closed each of the preceding periods. If we view these periods as successive attempts by the Spanish to respond to the realities of development under mercantile capitalism, the differences between the three periods and the significance of each period are even greater than Florescano implies. The first period, we suggest, represents the Spanish policy of instituting a dual society and a dual economy, as described above, in which the dominant Spanish sector attempted to skim tribute off the top of the dominated Indian sector. The second period represents Spanish attempts to overcome difficulties that developed during the first period. Between 1550 and 1579, the Spanish sought remedial measures which would in one way or another ensure the continuation of their initial policy of maintaining a dual economy, preserving the Indian economy as a source of wealth for both Indians and Spaniards. The third period then represents the total abandonment by the Spaniards of their vision of a dual economy. In place of their old policy, the Spanish substituted new provisions that were to result in or, more accurately, did in fact accompany the inevitable development of the Mexican economy and its agricultural sector as fully integrated parts of the world mercantile capitalist system.

The examination of the history of Mexican agriculture presented in the following chapters will be based on this overall analytical schema.

2 ❧ 1521-1548: the encomienda

During the first period after the conquest, that is until about 1548–9, the Spaniards sought to maintain the pre-hispanic organization of economic activity in Mexico. After replacing the Aztec rulers at the top of the pyramid, they appropriated tribute from this economy for themselves. José Miranda notes:

During the first decades of the colony the Spaniards were supplied principally by Indian tribute, either directly – the *encomenderos* [see below] – or indirectly, by purchase or exchange etc. Others were supplied in large part by the Indians through tribute...In the beginning, the Indians supplied large quantities of agricultural products – maize, beans, peppers, cocoa, etc. – and animals... and all sorts of other goods – lime, wood, chairs, kitchen utensils, blankets, charcoal etc...This lasted about a decade.   (Miranda 1952: 204)

Besides goods produced in the Indian sector of the economy, of course, the Indians supplied increasingly large quantities of labour to the Spaniards, who invested it and often the goods as well in numerous projects and enterprises of their own.

Nonetheless, the payment of tribute to the Spanish economy soon proved to be quite different from the payment of tribute to the previous Aztec lords. In the first place, the proportion of the economic surplus exacted from the Indians by the Spaniards that returned to the Indian economy in the form of social services and public investments was less than under Aztec rule. The Spaniards invested this surplus either in their own sector of the Mexican economy, or, worse still, they shipped a good part of it to the metropolis across the Atlantic from whence it found its way into the development of Western Europe. The contemporary Spanish friar, Alonso De Zorita, observed:

the Mexican kings and their allies, the Kings of Texcoco and Tacuba, left the natural lords of these provinces in command of all the land they conquered and acquired. This was true of the lesser as well as the supreme lords. They also allowed all the commoners to keep their land and property, and permitted them to retain their customs and practises and mode of government. The kings of Mexico, Texcoco, and Tacuba reserved for themselves certain lands which were cultivated for them by all the commoners. On these lands were grown the things that each region yielded. The conquered people did this by way of tribute and an acknowledgement of vassalship.   (Zorita 1965: 112)

In the second place, the number of people exempt from the payment of tribute declined as the Spanish tributory net became finer and finer. Zorita called attention to the fact that before the conquest

Those persons who did not hold land from their community or barrio, or preferred not to, rented it from some lord or other private party, or from some other barrio. The mayeques were serfs and paid tribute as such to the lord of the land that they occupied and worked. They had no such obligations to the supreme universal ruler, and paid him no tribute, but in time of war or need they were obliged to serve him in virtue of his universal dominion and the jurisdiction he had over them.   (Zorita 1964: 197)

These Indians and others, as Gibson (1964: 200) noted, lost their pre-hispanic exemptions from tribute and were now also deprived of their surplus.

In the third place, the amount of Spanish tribute apparently far exceeded the earlier Aztec tribute. Zorita wrote:

The third question asks the value of the tribute, expressed in gold pesos. This question is difficult to answer. [Before the conquest] each tribute payer gave but little, and that little had a low value for the Indians, but today it is worth a great deal. What I can state with certainty is that one Indian pays more tribute today than did six Indians at that time, and one town pays more in gold pesos today than did six towns of the kind that paid tribute in gold.
(Zorita 1965: 189)

In the fourth place, the tributory system quickly and increasingly became commercially integrated into the mercantile capitalist economy as a whole. Not only was the tribute collected by the Spaniards used in large part for commercial investment or sale, but the very collection of tribute – and in part through it the Indians themselves – quickly became commercialized and integrated into the economy as well. As early as 1532, some Indians asked to have the payment of the tribute they owed commuted from goods to money. A contemporary informed the king of this and asked him to remove the legal impediment to the payment of tribute in cash: 'Now it seems that in some places the Indians want to keep their maize and cloth for trading, and prefer to pay their tribute in gold, because through their trading they can earn enough to pay their tribute and to meet their subsistence needs' (Miranda 1952: 204). Apparently, in only ten years, inflation had taken hold of the new economy. Like all those who must pay in times of inflation, the Indians perceived the advantage of paying in devalued money instead of increasingly valuable goods. (We shall see that whenever landlords had to pay Indians and others since then, they chose to pay increasingly in money during times of inflation and in goods in times of deflation.) The Indians request was granted, and as long as labour was still in relatively plentiful supply even labour services were sometimes paid in money.

During this period also the Spanish acquisition of Mexican land began. During the conquest and the years immediately following, Cortés, with other military commanders and officials, took the initiative of distributing land amongst themselves and to others. In 1535 the king vested the viceroy with the legal right to give land grants (*mercedes*), with the provision that he could not make any grant to 'church, monastery, hospital or other ecclesiastical institution or person', as the repetition of this injunction in 1542 read (Chevalier 1970: 56–7). At this time, however, the Spanish population was still small and relied on the Indian economy for its agricultural supplies; hence land was of very little or no value to the Spaniards (Chevalier 1970: 55). It was of greater interest to the Indian chiefs and the Indian communities, who were also entitled to receive grants of land and who were in fact given such grants by the vice-regal authority. The real interest of the Spaniards, beyond the aforementioned goods produced by the Indian economy, was in Indian labour for use in the establishment and operation of Spanish enterprise. And the tributary payment of these labour services was, during the first colonial period, organized almost exclusively through the institution of the *encomienda*.

Arcila Farías writes:

The *encomienda* and property in land in [Latin] America are institutions which have nothing to do with each other. Among students of these institutions there is no confusion at all about the matter, and the specialist historians have put each thing in its proper place. In fact, there would be no justification for attempting here to clarify a question which is already quite clear, apart from the ignorance which exists in Venezuela about the *encomienda* as well as about the origins of property in land, as these have not yet been studied. Many people who write about history in our country frequently confuse the two terms and attribute the origins of property to the *encomienda*.

(Arcila Farías 1957: 307)

Unfortunately, this confusion continues to persist outside Venezuela as well.

The scholar who has done most to clear up this confusion is Silvio Zavala. In his *New Viewpoints on the Spanish Colonization of America* he writes:

The most generally accepted idea regarding the *encomienda* is that land and Indians were apportioned among the Spaniards in the first days of the conquest...but this notion that the *encomiendas* were the true origin of the *hacienda* is open to serious question, both in the light of the history of the land and of the history of the people...In summary, we may state that in New Spain property in the soil was not conveyed by granting of an *encomienda*. Within the boundaries of a single *encomienda* could be found lands held individually by the Indians; lands held collectively by the villagers; crown lands; lands acquired by the *encomendero* through a grant distinct from his title as *encomendero* or affected by his right to the payment of tribute in agricultural products; and lastly, lands granted to the Spaniards other than the *encomendero*. The foregoing demonstrates that the *encomienda* cannot have been the direct ancestor of the modern *hacienda* because the former did not involve true ownership.

(Zavala 1943: 80–4)

Indeed Zavala (1943: 84) and Miranda (1965: 27) have documented cases in which *encomenderos* solicited the viceroy for grants of land within the area of the Indians who owed them *encomienda* tribute. Some *encomenderos* were successful in using their influence to get such grants of land within their *encomienda*, despite the fact that the crown, which viewed the *encomenderos'* power as a threat to its own still weak authority in the Americas, discouraged such grants and took a dim view of them when they were made.

The institution of the *encomienda* and the *encomendero* or tribute recipient himself, besides being falsely associated with the institution of the *hacienda* that grew up at least two generations later, is often said to be feudal. Yet this characterization would not seem to be congruent with the *encomienda's* role in the collection of tribute (to be relayed overseas and channelled into the primitive capital accumulation of the developing mercantile capitalist capitalist system) or with the *encomenderos'* industrial and commercial activities within Mexico. According to Miranda:

The *encomendero* is above all a man who has time, who is moved by desire for profit and pursues the goal of wealth. Among his contemporaries, the *encomendero* is a man of action in whom the ideas and anxieties of a new world take strongest root . . . For that reason, he does not, like the feudal lord, limit himself to the mere enjoyment of tribute and service; but he converts the one like the other into the principal base of several business enterprises . . . He will do the same as any entrepreneur from that time till now; use his own and others' resources and the work of others in the pursuit of his own wealth and well-being. Thus, the *encomendero* gives pride of place to the capitalist grant element of *encomienda* which is the only one that can bring him what he pursues with vigour: riches . . . Therefore, at first, he dedicates himself entirely and above all to the exploitation of gold mines and to the production of related necessary articles (certain tools and materials), without forgetting the production of what is necessary to cover his most immediate needs (livestock and wheat). The businesses which the *encomendero* establishes to take economic advantage of the *encomienda* are therefore of three kinds: mining (for the extraction of gold, at first), livestock, and agriculture (agriculture, at first, being limited almost exclusively to the production of wheat) . . . With respect to mining, he would extract gold, the means of subsistence, slaves, clothing, etc. from his *encomienda* for his business. These goods will be used by him as follows: the gold, in the most necessary investment such as the purchase of tools, and where necessary in the payment of Spanish workers (miners and helpers) and the purchase of food; the means of subsistence in the maintenance of the slaves, *encomienda* Indians, and other workers, and livestock raising; the slaves in the mining work where they were the main source of labour, and in agriculture and livestock raising . . . We often see the *encomendero* caught up in a complicated net of economic and legal relationships; he participates in various mining companies, established before the public notary; he is owner of a herd of swine or sheep, which he grazes on the range of another *encomendero* – with whom he has entered into an economic contract for the purpose – and which are under the care of a Spaniard – whose services he has obtained through some contract or payment – and all this after having conferred general powers to some relative, friend, or employee to administer his *pueblos* and after having conferred special powers to other people so that they might administer his *hacienda* or livestock ranches, his shops or mills, or take care of his interests wherever it may be necessary.   (Miranda 1965: 10–11, 33–4)

Thus, though Miranda suggests that the *encomienda* combined some feudal elements with capitalist elements, it is undoubtedly the capitalist elements and more importantly the *encomendero's* full participation as an entrepreneur in a capitalist enterprise system which predominates (Miranda 1965: 5). Moreover, as Eric Wolf characterizes the *encomienda*, 'in the eyes of the colonist, it was not its medieval provenience which lent merit to the institution; it was rather the opportunity provided for the organization of a capitalist labor force over which he alone would exercise untrammelled sway' (Wolf 1959: 189).

By 1560, New Spain counted 480 *encomenderos* who between them exacted a tribute of 377,734 pesos. By then, the *encomienda* as the principal institution for harnessing Indian labour to the Spanish mercantilist economy had already passed its golden years and was being replaced by new institutions. Indian slavery and *encomienda* tribute, combined with European diseases against which Indians lacked immunity, wrought havoc on the Indian population and its social organizations, despite the abolition of slavery in 1535 and the royal and viceregal limitation of *encomienda* abuses through restrictions – which more often than not remained dead letters. For example, the fixing by the authorities after 1536 of the amount of tribute to be paid to the *encomenderos*; the prohibitions against the use of *encomienda* labour in mining, cattle herding, and the construction of houses for sale, and against the rental or lending of *encomienda* labour to others; and the placing of an upper limit of twenty days on the period that an Indian could legally be made to be absent from his home. The very existence of these restrictions and their repetition in one viceregal ordinance after another suggests the widespread violation of their provisions and the far-reaching abuse of Indian labour by the Spanish colonists. Moreover, Indian chiefs who received tribute in kind and labour from their subjects – in part as tribute collectors for the Spaniards and in part as recipients of tribute in their own right – now used it increasingly for their personal benefits as though they were any other *encomendero*, which indeed they essentially were under Spanish law. The Indian nobles, suggests Wolf, like other *encomenderos,* began to invest in the process of building capital through capitalist enterprise. Frequently, intermarriage with the conquerors still further dissipated their Indian identity, until they lost touch with the Indian commoners who in the midst of death and upheaval were building a new Indian life in the countryside...Thus the Indians suffered not only exploitation and biological collapse but also deculturation – cultural loss – and in the course of such ill use lost also the feeling of belonging to a social order which made such poor use of its human resources. They became strangers in it, divided from its purposes and agents by an abyss of distrust. The new society could command their labor, but it could not command their loyalty. Nor has this gulf healed in the course of time. The trauma of the Conquest remains an open wound on the body of Middle American society to this day.

(Wolf 1959: 212–14)

The only escape from the payment of tribute was death – available to many – or moving out of the Indian communities into the sparsely settled high lands – possible only for the relatively few.

3 ❧ 1548-1575: the *repartimiento*

The second period of colonization begins after the epidemic of 1545 to 1548. This epidemic was responsible for the death of perhaps a fourth to a third of the Indian population and placed severe strains on the Mexican economy, particularly on the colonists' attempts to maintain a division into an Indian and a Spanish sector. The second period, then, may be said to represent Spanish attempts to face this crisis, while still remaining within the conception of a duality of the economy and a separation between the Spanish and Indian sectors. The most notable of these efforts were the rapid expansion of the Spanish sector of the economy, the introduction of the *repartimiento* labour draft and the extension of tribute collection through taxation by the *corregimiento* or civil administration (which together were coming increasingly to replace the *encomienda*), and various attempts to increase the production and delivery of agricultural commodities by the Indian sector.

Continued Spanish interest in the preservation and productive contribution of the Indian sector is evident from measures such as the following. In 1558 the viceregal authorities ordered that all available lands within the Indian sector be used for production. *Mercedes*, or land grants, were made to Indian towns and to Indian chiefs, as well as to Spaniards. In 1556 the tribute payments which, at the Indians' request, had been commuted from payment in kind to payment in money after 1532, were again ordered to be delivered in maize and other goods in an attempt to meet the shortage of 1555. In 1559, in an attempt to encourage the cultivation of wheat, the Spaniards required tribute of this cereal (Florescano 1965a: 583). Especially after

15

1564, declining deliveries of maize were met by viceregal attempts to force the Indians to deliver this crop to the cities. Furthermore, Spaniards were forbidden to buy Indian maize except in publicly supervised markets. Indians were also asked to deliver chickens. Perhaps most important of all, the Spanish authorities tried to protect the Indian and his economy by decreeing in 1567 that each Indian town be reserved the land surrounding it for 500 *varas* (about 370 metres) in all directions and that no Spanish cattle ranch might come within 1,000 *varas* of such towns.

The allocation of economic activities between the Spanish and Indian sectors seems to have been determined primarily, as Eric Wolf points out, by their relative profitability, which in turn depended in large part on their relative requirements in terms of capital and labour (Wolf 1959: 180–81). Thus, the Spaniards increasingly reserved for themselves mining, manufacturing, the large-scale commercial activities other than agriculture, as well as wheat farming, cattle ranching, and the production of such commercial crops as sugar and indigo. That is to say, these enterprises were in Spanish hands. The labour, of course, was provided by Indians and to a minor extent by Negro slaves; and all Spanish primitive capital accumulation was derived from Indian tribute. The Indian sector was left to raise maize, vegetables, farmyard animals, and to provide things like firewood. Among commercial crops, the Indians were allocated the production of cotton, silk, cacao, and cochineal dye, all of whose production was highly labour-intensive. Nonetheless, the profitable commercialization of these products was largely reserved for the Spaniards.

Viewed geographically, as Pierre Chaunu has suggested, the Mexican economy came to grow along two axes, east–west and north–south. The east–west axis, passing through Veracruz–Mexico–Acupulco, was the Mexican leg of the Spanish global commercial axis passing through Cuba and the Antilles to Spain in the west and extending through the Philippines to China in the east. Beyond its empire-wide commercial significance, this axis was also of considerable productive significance in Mexico itself. It included, of course, the capital of Mexico, the populous, irrigated Valley of Mexico, and the important agricultural and especially wheat-growing areas of the valleys of Atlixco, Puebla and Tlaxcala, as well as the sugar-growing valley of Cuernavaca, all of which were opened to Spanish commercial agriculture not long after the conquest. The north–south axis, still called the Camino Real, extended farther and farther north, as more and more mining and cattle areas were opened up and integrated into the world mercantile capitalist economy. Towards the south, this axis ran through the fertile valleys of Oaxaca into the highlands of Chiapas, which then belonged to the captaincy of Guatemala. The axes crossed in the capital. After dispatching its share of tribute to the metropolis overseas, Mexico City fed on what remained of the economic surplus extracted along these axes from the rest of Mexico (and indeed from other parts of the Spanish empire).

Spanish agricultural production and distribution was commercial from the very beginning. The Spanish staple was wheat. Wheat production increased gradually during the first decades after the conquest as the Spanish population and productive capacity grew. The price of wheat declined in Mexico from 1529–42 as the supply increased, while the price rose in Spain and less, presumably, was available for export from the mother country (Chevalier 1970: 62). Then, for a while, the price of wheat and flour remained more or less stable in Mexico. Beginning in the mid-1550s, the price of wheat began the rise that was to last the remainder of that century and into the seventeenth century. This price rise may be attributed to three principal factors: the increased quantity of wheat demanded by a growing Spanish population, the increased supply price due to shortages of Indian labour available for wheat farming, and a general inflation associated with an increase in the supply of money derived from the growing output of the Mexican silver mines. In the capital the price of a *fanega* of wheat increased from three to six *reales* in the 1540s to about twelve *reales* in the latter part of the 1550s (Chevalier 1970: 62). By 1580, after another major epidemic (see below), the price had risen to around twenty or twenty-two *reales* (Florescano 1965a: 599). In the newly opened mining areas of Nueva Galicia the price rise was astronomical: the discovery of silver in Zacatecas in 1548 drove up the price in the whole region. In Guadalajara the price of wheat quintupled in the three years from 1547–50. The price of maize jumped ten times during the same years. In Zacatecas itself, the price of maize was six times higher still, so that the Zacatecas price in 1550 was sixty times higher than the Guadalajara price in 1547, before the silver strike (Chevalier 1970: 63). And at the minehead in San Martin the price of maize in the 1550s was another ten times higher than in Zacatecas, or a full six hundred times higher than it had been in Guadalajara in 1547.

This increase in the demand for and the price of wheat, and later of maize, increased their commercial profitability – and that in turn called for new, larger-scale, Spanish wheat enterprises which demanded and received Indian labour and land which had been Indian. The Valley of Mexico alone came to count 115 commercial Spanish wheat farms, which produced for the Mexico City market. At that time most of these grew thirty to sixty *fanegas* of wheat, although some were as large as 200 to 400 *fanegas* (Florescano 1965a: 584). A still more important centre of Spanish commercial wheat farming was the valley at Atlixco and the neighbouring regions of Puebla and Tlaxcala. These supplied not only the Mexico City market, but also that of the growing city of Puebla; and they shipped wheat to Veracruz to supply the Spanish merchant fleet when it landed there. The astronomical prices of wheat and other commodities in the new mining regions attest both to the costliness of shipping so bulky a commodity to those far-off areas of consumption and to the profitability of developing new sources of supply close at hand. Spanish entrepreneurs were quick to begin cultivation in the north to meet this demand and to take advantage of such opportunity for profit.

Another commercial crop grown and processed by Spanish capitalist enterprises was sugar. The valleys of Cuernavaca, Zacatepec–Jojutla, and Cuaútla in Morelos, the home state of Emiliano Zapata, soon became the centre of Mexico's sugar industry, as they have remained to this day. Cortés planted sugar for the world market immediately after the conquest, first near

Córdoba and then around Cuernavaca (Sandoval 1951: 42). It was not uncommon for several Spaniards to get together to form companies to grow and process sugar so that they might raise the large capital investment necessary by pooling the financial resources and the Indian *encomienda* and African slave labour at their command. Indeed, this had been Spanish practice since the beginning of the sixteenth century, and in the New World it had already been followed in Santo Domingo in 1516 (Sandoval 1951: 111). In 1539 the Marqués del Valle (that is, Cortés) joined with another Spaniard to found the first company to produce sugar (it owned a plantation and a mill) in the present state of Morelos. The establishment of such companies plus the high capital requirement and profitability of the sugar industry encouraged other commercial activities. Sandoval notes:

The large amount of credit that individuals and particularly religious institutions granted to the sugar plantations during the whole of the vice-regency, despite the fact that these continually changed hands as their owners failed to repay loans, shows that the sugar industry was economically profitable and that it developed successfully in New Spain...[E]ven though the industrialists went bankrupt on the average of every eight to ten years, their creditors continued to have confidence in the sugar industry and went on supporting it because they considered it able to guarantee their loans.
(Sandoval 1951: 114, 117)

One of the important sources of credit for the sugar industry was the Real Fisco de la Inquisición, that is the Treasury of the Inquisition (Sandoval 1951: 118–19). Another commercial instrument of the industry was the practice by some owners of sugar plantations (who did not work them themselves) of renting their plantations for a flat fee to others who undertook the risk and earned the profit of working the plantation and mill. The first owner to rent his sugar plantation in this way was the second Marqués de Valle, Martin Cortés, in 1566 (Sandoval 1951: 111).

Furthermore, as we shall see below, many sugar plantations rented part of the land they used from Indians. Sugar plantations already encroached on wheat lands in 1547–8 and on maize lands throughout their first period of expansion which lasted into the 1570s. Sugar production then levelled off and even declined in Mexico, in large part because of official intervention, until a new increase in the early seventeenth century (Moreno Toscano 1965: 646). This official intervention was prompted in part by the Spanish view of its empire as a whole, which in this case resulted in the stimulation of sugar production in the Spanish Caribbean and its limitation in New Spain; and it was reinforced after the epidemic of 1576 by viceregal intervention in market allocation of resources in accordance with private profitability when, in the opinion of the authorities, grain supplies and the profitable sugar industry competed unduly for land and labour.

Another commercial commodity produced by the Spanish, particularly in Yucatan and Guatemala, was indigo. The Spaniards also introduced livestock into New Spain – first pigs, and then successively sheep and cattle. Pigs were introduced by Cortés shortly after the conquest, and they were fed on tribute maize. The supply of pigs increased so much that the price of an *arrelde* of pork fell from six *maravedís* in 1524 to one half *maravedi* in 1532 (Matesánz 1965: 535–7). Grazing often on virgin lands (though, as we will see below, there was also much invasion of Indian crop lands), the livestock herds multiplied rapidly. The supply of meat available was reflected in its price, as the cost of an *arrelde* of meat fell from seventeen *maravedís* in 1538, to twelve in 1539, to ten in 1540, to seven in 1541, to four in 1542. In that same year, the price of meat in Andalucía was seven to eight times higher than in Mexico. The city council of Mexico even fixed a minimum price for meat in an attempt to stop further depreciation. Prices stabilized, but more because the livestock herds stopped growing after the middle of the century than because of official interference. In the 1550s and 1560s the price of meat hovered around six *maravedís*, and by 1575 it had risen to eight to nine *maravedís* per *arrelde* (Chevalier 1970: 85, 104). As well as breeding livestock for meat, the raising of mules and horses for the transport of goods and men became another profitable enterprise, especially as the northern mines and associated agricultural regions were opened.

Florescano summarizes this development of the Spanish agricultural sector:

Until 1550, agriculture rested entirely upon the effort and initiative of the Indians, with some exceptions. After that time, the decline of the native population, the increase of the European population, of the urban centres and the mining camps and the consolidation of Spanish power generated the development of a Spanish-run, commercial agriculture, specializing in wheat and, in exceptional cases, maize (in Puebla, around Mexico City and in the north of New Spain). This type of agriculture is established on fertile lands which have abundant water and which are located in strategic points and places: for example, near the large consumer centres (Mexico City), along highways in distribution areas such as Puebla, Guadalajara–Zacatecas highway etc.), or around the mining centres (Zacatecas, Parral, Guanajuato, etc). Furthermore, this kind of agriculture, run and managed by the Spaniards, was of course, more productive and used better agricultural techniques. We are dealing, then, with the first example of commercial agriculture to appear in New Spain ... this new agriculture devoted its production to supplying the principal consumer centres in New Spain at that time – cities (Mexico, Puebla), mining camps and ports (Veracruz, Campeche, Havana) – where wheat, flour or maize were in great demand and commanded a high price.

(Florescano 1965a: 591–2)

The development in the north is summarized by Chevalier:

In the sixteenth century, all those *ricos homes* who did not owe their start to public office owed it wholly or in part of the mines or, frequently, to trade, never, unlike their fellows in New Spain, to rich encomiendas. Agriculture and livestock, which were to be their subsequent source of capital, did not count in the beginning; they were merely a necessity in order to supply the mines with food. Then agriculture and livestock became a way to invest earned income – a most tempting one, because food and beasts of burden were bringing very high prices in the new mining centers. (Chevalier 1970: 165)

The development of the Spanish agriculture, like that of the remainder of the Spanish economy, required capital. Since the colonists brought no Spanish capital to speak of with them, this capital had to be supplied by the Indians in the form of land, labour, tribute or taxes, and through trading profit. Though the Spanish attempt to foster a dual economy persisted, the exigencies of filling and even pursuing these requirements increasingly integrated the two sectors of the economy into a single economy of commercial capitalist structure and development. Spanish acquisition of Indian land was organized less and less through simple royal grant and more and more through the purchase and the economically or politically forced sale or abandonment of Indian lands. After the epidemic of 1545–8, which wiped out a fourth to a third of the Indian population, 'the uneconomical labor institutions of the first colonial years would no longer suffice' as Gibson notes (1964: 224). The tributary functions of the *encomienda* as a labour draft were increasingly taken over by a new labour institution, the *repartimiento*. The exaction of tribute in the form of goods and money through the *encomienda* continued; but it was now frequently superseded by the collection of tribute through head taxes, which the *corregimiento* or civil government placed on the whole Indian population. The tax collectors became 'tax farmers' who operated like other merchants with monopoly powers, and who also expanded their activities in other directions.

The three principal ways in which the Spaniards acquired land from the Indians are summarized by Gibson (1964: 274–5). These testify to the commercial significance of land in the monopolistic capitalist society which was already emerging immediately after the conquest. The first method of acquiring land was purchase. This practice and the commercial integration of agriculture that it brought with it was introduced even before the conquest was completed, and it has been in use ever since. Of course, in a market in which economic and political power is highly concentrated such purchase is often little better than extortion and often the purchase is combined with fraud, in that the purchaser knowingly deceives the seller about the value of the land and/or the payment. The second method was to rely on one's authority and power as an *encomendero* or political official to extort favours or concessions from the holders of land. Sometimes these two methods were combined in the occupation of Indian land whose owners had been driven off by economic or political pressure or simply by violence and which, both in the sixteenth century and again in the nineteenth century was then 'denounced' as vacant and available for occupation by another owner.

The third method of acquiring land was through the receipt of a *merced* or grant of land, first from the conquering generals or municipal authority and after 1535 from the viceroy. In the beginning pasture land was not subject to such grants: it was in fact protected by measures such as those prohibiting the raising of fences. Nonetheless, pasture land was increasingly acquired by the Spaniards; and the viceregal authorities subsequently found themselves obliged to extend legal recognition to this occupation of pasture land and even to make further grants. These grants became so large that, though they were smaller in number than the grants of agricultural land, the total area of pasture land allocated in this way was larger than that of agricultural land. Thus by no means all of the land acquired by the Spaniards was acquired through *mercedes*; nor was this land exempt from the early commercialization of the Mexican agricultural economy. More often than not, the land received in *merced* was immediately augmented by the purchase of additional land (Gibson 1964: 289). Moreover, the *mercedes* themselves were subject to speculation; so much so, that already in 1561 speculation on *mercedes* was denounced. In 1563, to combat this development, the viceroy prohibited the sale of any part of land received less than three years earlier, on pain of losing all of the land so granted. Like most of these viceregal provisions, this one was not enforced; and in 1567 the 'thousand evils and thousand sales and resales' of *mercedes* were denounced again. As a consequence, by the seventeenth century *mercedes* were often accompanied by a licence for immediate sale of the land so received (Chevalier 1970: 135).

The other and by far the most important source of Spanish capital accumulation was Indian labour. The epidemic of 1545–8 wiped out as we have seen a fourth to a third of the Indian population and ushered in a new labour institution that was to replace the *encomienda*. As Gibson suggests, 'the uneconomical institutions of the first colonial years would no longer suffice' (Gibson 1964: 224). On 22 February 1549 the king issued a *cedula* prohibiting the payment of *encomienda* tribute through labour services. According to Silvio Zavala, this law was enforced (Zavala 1943: 85). Henceforth *encomienda* tribute was paid only in money or in kind, and the *encomienda* ceased to be an institution for the Spanish mobilization of Indian labour. The labour tribute of the *encomienda* was replaced by the labour draft of an institution variously called *repartimiento, rueda, tanda, cuatequil*, or in Peru *mita*.

The decline in the supply of Indian labour after the epidemic of 1545–8, the increase in the demand for labour by the Spanish sector of the economy (which included increasing public and private claimants for labour in those who had no *encomienda* or hopes of getting one), and the general development of the economy required the development of a labour institution that would be more efficient in catching communal Indians in the Spanish labour net and allocating them to a larger and changing number of Spanish demands – a labour institution, in short, that would be at once more productive and more flexible. Silvio Zavala asks: 'Through what channels would the labour necessary for carrying on the work of the colony now be obtained?' And he answers:

The aim... was to establish a system of voluntary wage labour with moderate tasks; but in anticipation that the Indians might not offer their services voluntarily... [the Spanish instituted] the *cuatequil* or the system of forced wage labour. This system, combined with the previous indigenous customs, was to develop on a much larger scale in Peru under the name of *mita*, an institution distinct from both slavery and the personal service on the *encomienda*, both of which were disappearing in the process we are describing... The Indians received a daily wage... the main differences between the *cuatequil* of New Spain and the *mita* of Peru lay in the fact that the former usually affected the Indians in districts near their place of work, while in Peru the labourers had to travel much greater distances. In New Spain the work period was almost always one week and each Indian presented himself for work three or four weeks a year. Peruvian periods of labour lasted for four months. The quota of workers raised by the villages of New Spain was commonly 4%, in Peru one-seventh or about 14%; in Tucumán one Indian was taken out of twelve... a system of compulsory wage labour... in the end it became the chief source of labour in the colony. Not even the *encomendero* succeeded in remaining independent of the institution of the *cuatequil*. If they needed labourers they could no longer take them directly from their villages, as they had formerly done, as a form of tribute. Like other private colonists, they were forced to apply to a justice of *juez repartidor* for the number of Indians they needed and the workers thus provided no longer worked gratuitously but were entitled to customary wages from the *encomendero*.

(Zavala 1943: 93–7)

Gibson describes the *repartimiento* in the Valley of Mexico:

The word means distribution or apportionment, and it was applied to a series of diverse colonial procedures, including encomienda grants, land allotment, tribute apportionment, forced sale, and draft labour. For the moment, we adopt the most common usage of the sixteenth and seventeenth centuries, identifying as repartimiento the institution that dominated the recruitment of Indian workers for a period of about seventy-five years after the mid-century. It was a system of rationed, rotational labor, purportedly in the public interest or for the public utility, affecting both encomienda and non-encomienda

Indians, and benefiting a much larger employer class than had been possible under encomienda. In fact, it did not fulfil the royal demands for short hours, moderate tasks, or voluntary labor for wages. But it subjected the labor procedures of the colony to administrative scrutiny for the first time, and it satisfied, at least temporarily, the needs of the new colonial employers.

(Gibson 1964: 224)

In agriculture for the first three decades the quota of labour demanded of each Indian community was about 1% of its working population during the *sencilla* period of November to April, and 2% during the *dobla* growing season from May to October (Gibson 1964: 231). This amounted to about 6.3% of the Indians' annual working time (Borah 1951: 35–6). Especially after the epidemic of 1575, the *Jueces repartidores*, who allocated this Indian labour to the Spanish employers, increased the labour draft on their own authority to meet the growing labour shortage. Late in the sixteenth century the viceroy came to authorize drafts of 5% during the *sencilla* and 8% during the *dobla* (Gibson 1964: 232). The Indians were paid wages for the time they worked but not for their travel time, which was not included in the earlier quotas either, despite the fact that travel time often was as long as working time.

The *repartimiento* was an integral part of the mercantile capitalist organization of the economy, despite being an institution of forced labour. One indication of this integration is the above-cited increase in the labour draft quotas in response to decreases in the labour supply. Another is that as the supply of labour decreased, the working and nutritional conditions of *repartimiento* Indians improved (Borah and Cook 1962: 7). In fact the very substitution of the *repartimiento* for the *encomienda* as the institution of labour allocation represented an improvement in Indian labour conditions in response to increased demand and decreased supply of labour. Thirdly, money wages increased for *repartimiento* labourers as demand for labour increased and its supply decreased. Before 1549, when the *repartimiento* was incipient and the *encomienda* still produced tribute in the form of labour services, the daily *repartimiento* wage was one quarter of a *real*. By 1553 it had risen to half a *real*. In the 1560s it was two thirds of a *real*, and during the 1570s it rose to three quarters of a *real*. In 1590 the wage reached one *real*, during the first decade of the seventeenth century one and a half *reales*, and by 1629 it was two *reales*. None-theless, the element of force is also reflected in the *repartimiento* wage: hiring a substitute for *repartimiento* labour cost up to twice the current *repartimiento* wage (Gibson 1964: 249–50). This implies that although the principle of supply and demand was in operation, the same distribution of property and income would have evoked a higher wage in the absence of the compulsory feature of the labour draft.

Associated with Spanish appropriation of Indian land and labour during the second half of the sixteenth century was another institution, the *congregación*. This institution involved the resettlement of Indians in new communities, often on less suitable lands. These new communities were established to replace existing ones which had become depopulated through death or migration and also to provide sources of labour in regions where there was a growing demand for labour. The Mexican *congregación* was patterned on a similar institution initiated by Viceroy Toledo in Peru in 1569–71. In Mexico, however, the *congregación* was not widely resorted to until the closing years of the sixteenth century.

The number of Indians who were resettled in Mexico through the *congregación* has been estimated at half a million, and perhaps at only a quarter of a million by 1605 (Cline 1949: 367). Cline terms this 'a rather small fraction of the known native families' (1949: 367). But if we compare the mid-point of his estimate (i.e. a third of a million Indians) with the estimates of the total Indian population for 1605 and 1607 of about one million (Borah and Cook 1962: 5) or two million (Borah 1951: 2), we find a third or a sixth of the Indian population to have been resettled. Even allowing for the population decline that is attributable to the *congregación* itself (since the population totals used for comparison are the end of period totals), this population resettlement is considerable by the standards of modern colonization schemes. Moreover, the *congregación* was terminated at the turn of the century, perhaps because at that time the growth of mining in the North ceased and its exploitation began to decline.

The contribution of the *congregación* to the Spanish control of Indian labour was that it concentrated the supply of that labour so as to facilitate the imposition and exaction of the labour quota and perhaps of the tributory tax in both goods and money. The *congregación* was related to Spanish land acquisition in that it removed Indians from lands that were in demand by the Spaniards themselves. These lands were 'denounced' as vacant and were added to the expanding Spanish farms.

However, both the acquisition of land and labour by the Spanish (and by Indian chiefs) and the collection of Indian tribute in other forms came to be increasingly organized through other institutions. As the Spanish economy expanded and particularly as the absolute and relative importance of the *encomienda* declined, the exaction of tribute in kind and money was increasingly taken over by the civil government, or *corregimiento*, which imposed head taxes on the non-*encomienda* Indians, who were regarded as being *encomendado* to the king. Nonetheless, the civil and judicial jurisdiction of the *corregimiento* was soon extended to *encomienda* Indians also. Though the *corregidores* were formally civil officials, their economic functions appear increasingly to have outweighed their civil ones. Gibson summarizes:

Corregimientos were in demand among would-be officeholders to the extent that they offered favorable circumstances for business and finance. Like the encomenderos before them, the corregidores performed economic functions of far-reaching implications, and, as in encomienda, a substantial portion of the burden fell upon the Indian community. In this respect three features of the late [colonial, but to a lesser extent also sixteenth-century] corregimiento deserve mention: tribute collection, *derramas*, and commerce.

Colonial law made corregidores responsible for the delivery of tribute to the treasury officers, but it forbade their making collections directly from Indian tributaries. The reasons have to do with the corregidores' known propensity to divert tribute funds into their own pockets. Corregidores did receive food and goods from Indians, however, and from the start their practice was to sell these materials for profit. According to a viceregal statement, embezzlement of tribute funds had become a common corregidor's procedure by the seventeenth century.

The term derrama, in its colonial usage, refers to extra or unauthorized tributes. Exaction of derramas was not an exclusive device of the corregidores – clergymen and local Indian officials were also adept in this – but it consistently served corregidores as a means of raising money. Fees for the performance of official duties and fines for transgressions of the law were closely associated with derramas...

The corregidors' interest in commerce appears in part as an outgrowth of the concern with tribute and with derramas. As recipients of Indian payments and with access to a variety of commodities, the early corregidores enjoyed some particular commercial advantages...Colonial law belatedly listed and ineffectively forbade the enterprises into which corregidores were known to be expanding: the marketing of wheat and maize, the marketing of chickens and other fowl, the raising of pigs and cattle, farming, and the ownership of land...The corregidor's common procedure was to buy cheaply, often from Indians themselves (a method not greatly different from levying a derrama), and then to make a forced distribution (repartimiento), again to Indians, at inflated prices.   (Gibson 1964: 93–4).

The commercialization of tribute collection and payment is evident, and through this, as well as in other ways, the progressive incorporation of the entire population and its agricultural pursuits into the mercantile capitalist economy.

The function of tribute and its changing institutional organization is aptly summarized by Gibson:

In sum, the tribute obligation was a continuing annual burden for the Indian communities. Tribute represented a direct exaction, a device through which in its initial stage a privileged Spanish class, and subsequently the Spanish political state, obtained a calculated revenue from the Indian population. Two major developments of the sixteenth century were the decay of encomienda tribute and the intensification, or Hispanization, of the rules relating to liability and payment. These were consistent with the sixteenth-century changes in Indian class structure, as well as with the imperial government's increasing financial needs. Spaniards rarely collected tributes directly from the local Indian taxpayers. Instead, Indian officers were the intermediaries and the ones held answerable in instances of default. The procedure allowed Spanish government to remain aloof from the petty tasks of collection and to concentrate on a relatively small number of Indian leaders who could easily be held accountable. It allowed also for some perpetuation of ancient Indian practices, including the graduated liabilities based on rank or land, which ran counter to Spanish head-tax assessments. Moreover, it reinforced the authority of Indian town governments, which were able to collect in excess of the assessments and to exploit the payers. But when this authority proved insufficient, the result was an accumulation of community debts, punishable through jail sentences. Finally there was an intimate connection between tribute and community finance. Because a fraction of the tribute was assigned to the town governments for local expenses and support of the clergy, both Spanish and Indian revenues became linked with the Indian community organization.   (Gibson 1964: 219)

The Spanish economy in Mexico was, of course, an extension and integral part of the mercantile capitalist economy of the metropolis. Already in the 1560s, the marketing of agricultural products in the Spanish economy was entirely commercialized; and the economy already displayed the monopolistic and speculative features that it has retained to this day. (We will see below how, through its ties with the Indian economy, the Spanish economy drew the former into this network as well and stamped it with the same features.) Until about 1552–5, Indian merchandise tribute was transported to the cities at the Indians' expense and delivered to the Spanish there. After 1555 Indian merchandise tribute was more and more frequently handed over in the villages themselves; and the cost of transportation to the city was born by the recipient. At first sight, this change might appear as a reduction of the Indians' burden. In fact, this change in the point of delivery brought the middleman, who had previously confined his activities principally to the Spanish cities, right to the Indians' doorstep. And with the middleman, of course, came speculation. The price of maize, which was already rising due to the circumstances reviewed earlier, was driven still higher by this expansion of the field for monopolistic and speculative middleman activity (Florescano 1965a: 573). Once the middlemen got to the villages, they expanded their activities and began to advance crop loans to the Indian producers in order to assure themselves of a supply of goods and to extend their control over the producers themselves (Florescano 1965a: 575). The Spanish viceregal and municipal authorities opposed this middleman and speculative activity, which often resulted in price mark-ups of several hundred per cent (Gibson 1964: 360). But, excepting the severe control measures adopted in times of crisis (like those following the epidemic of 1575 to which we shall turn below), official Spanish opposition was essentially ineffectual. Gonzalo Gomez de Cervantes wrote a few years later:

This process has gone to such extremes that middleman speculation is accepted freely and openly as if it were a good thing, since nothing which enters this city of Mexico may be bought directly by a citizen, rather it passes first into the hands of middlemen who resell it to us and who are not content to earn a hundred per cent on this change of hands but insist on such excessive profit that they take four hundred per cent and even more from us.   (cited in Florescano 1965a: 609)

The Spanish conception of a dual economy with separate Indian and Spanish sectors thus persisted even through the second period of colonization. It was even accompanied by royal and viceregal attempts to protect the Indians through legislation and other means. But as Chevalier (1970: 206) suggests, the viceroys would have needed much more power than they had to protect the Indians against the ravages of Spanish mercantile capitalist expansion. More significantly, their principal task, of course, was not to protect the Indians but to supervise and facilitate the functioning of this same system and its expansion. During this second period of sixteenth-century colonization, the expanding economy necessarily penetrated deeper and deeper into the Indian economy, which was increasingly converted into an integral appendage of the economy as a whole. Like everyone else, the viceregal authorities found themselves obliged increasingly to adjust to the logic of these events.

The effects of the Spanish economic expansion on the Indian agricultural economy were various, but all of them were profound. Florescano summarizes one of these effects:

> The appropriation of the best lands by the Spaniards, and sometimes their mere presence, obliged the Indians to install themselves in regions of retreat [*refugio*]. Thus, the irrigated lands and the main valleys, (Mexico, Toluca, Puebla) were incorporated little by little into the new agriculture while the Indians withdrew to the mountainous and least accessible regions. There, in fact, on the hillsides, they could apply their traditional agricultural methods more efficiently...[The Indian] remained tied to a subsistence agriculture, based on maize, beans, and chili peppers; his isolation protected his community's husbandry from contact, but at the same time it kept him from the agricultural technology introduced by the European.
>
> (Florescano 1965a: 592–3)

That is to say, as Florescano notes elsewhere, they did not so much maintain as 'develop systems of subsistence consumption' (Florescano 1965a: 592, 578). But the commercial expansion which deprived the Indian of his principal means of production, the land, also robbed him of other instruments of production and, through tribute and other means, of much of the income that resulted from his labour. The mercantile capitalist expansion thus forced into economic retrenchment even those Indians who did not retreat physically, because by remaining in the valleys and within physical reach of the Spaniards they exposed themselves to the consequent reduction in their income and purchasing power. Florescano notes in this respect:

The needs of the European in the city little by little destroyed the commercial development that Cortés and Bernal Diaz del Castillo had admired when they observed the intense activity of the markets of Tenochtitlan–Tlatelolco...there was a notable decline in transactions and in consequence a turn to less developed systems of exchange. (Florescano 1965a: 578)

Nonetheless, as Gibson notes, 'The Spanish monetary system rapidly became an element in Indian life, and again the principal impetus was tribute. Caciques, merchants, wealthy Indians, and the officers responsible for community finance developed as sophisticated an appreciation of Spanish money as any colonist' (Gibson 1964: 357). Indeed, it was this very incorporation of the Indian in the Spanish monetary (that is, mercantile capitalist) system which forced many Indians to live at or even below subsistence level. As we saw earlier, Indians had already in 1532 requested that they be permitted to pay their tribute in money instead of in goods. In 1556, presumably due to food shortages, the viceroy ordered that Indians again be required to pay their tribute in goods, particularly maize, instead of money. In 1559 the Indians were ordered to deliver wheat as part of their tribute, in an attempt to encourage them to grow wheat. The monetarization of the Indian economy is indicated by the fact that in 1561 this order had to be rescinded again, because it was found that, instead of producing more wheat, the Indians bought the required wheat from the Spaniards on the market and turned around to deliver it back to them in the form of tribute (Florescano 1965a: 583). When for similar reasons Viceroy Velasco ordered the Indians to supply chickens in 1592, he was forced to abolish the requirement in 1601 because the tributary Indians also went to the market to buy chickens for their tribute payments instead of producing them themselves (Gibson 1964: 204). Far from increasing the supply of wheat and chickens available or reducing their price, as intended, these measures did the opposite; both viceroys were obliged to adapt to the contradictory realities of the capitalist economic organization, which had long since penetrated both the Indian and the Spanish economies and fused them together. During the 1550s and 1560s numerous viceregal efforts to increase Indian production and delivery of maize by resorting to various administrative regulations met with similar lack of success (Gibson 1964: 326). Such viceregal measures and their inefficacy show that the Spanish conception of a dual economy persisted even when the existence of a single but contradictory capitalist economy was increasingly evident.

Spanish physical and commercial incursion upon the Indian economy took multiple forms and had various consequences. Though the decline in the Indian population of all regions was large, the gulf coast region especially became severely depopulated (Borah and Cook 1962: 9). In consequence, Indian economic activity on or near the coast also declined (Florescano 1965b: 66). This decline was particularly marked in the production of cotton. Not only was much of the basis of lowland cotton production destroyed, but the market for cotton declined as it came to be increasingly replaced by wool from the sheep which the Spaniards grazed on Indian lands in the centre of Mexico (Borah and Cook 1962: 9). Similarly, the production of cacao also declined after 1540. The decline also was due only in part to the attrition of population. Spanish imperial policy was to regard the empire as a single whole and to encourage specialization of production in its various parts. The production of cacao, silk and other commodities was administratively discouraged in the south–east of Mexico and encouraged initially in Guatemala and later in Venezuela and Ecuador. Indeed the costs of producing cacao in South America appear to have been lower than they were further north, for as the centre of production moved south between 1605 and 1625 the price of cacao in the capital of Mexico declined by more than one half, despite the increase in distance from the point of supply (Gibson 1964: 349). At the same time Oaxaca became, along with Guatemala, the principal supplier of cochineal for the production of red dyes. The dye-yielding insects were collected by Indians who worked largely for themselves but depended on the Spaniards for commercialization of the product. Until artificial dyes replaced cochineal on the world market two hundred years later, the production of cochineal, primarily in Oaxaca but also in Puebla and Tlaxcala, provided Mexico's largest source of export income after silver.

As well as taking Indian land, the expansion of Spanish agriculture and of the economy in general also appropriated and even destroyed Indian sources of water and firewood. Thus, the Spaniards not only appropriated irrigated lands, but they took care to get the springs which supplied water for irrigation and the canals which transported it (Gibson 1964: 280, Wolf 1959: 199). Moreover, the struggle to appropriate previously communal irrigation works into private property often destroyed some of the canals themselves or interfered with their maintenance. The fuel needs of Spanish enterprises, particularly sugar and are refineries where these existed, seriously encroached upon the Indians' supply of firewood; and Spanish expansion even deprived them of the hills themselves from which the firewood came, but where the Indians had also come to graze their animals.

The greatest physical damage to Indian agriculture, however, was done by the expansion of Spanish livestock ranching. The spectacular natural increase of cattle and sheep herds in the middle of the sixteenth century literally overran not only Indian pastures but also their crop lands. 'Sheep ate men' in Mexico just as they did during the enclosures in England (Wolf 1959: 198, Florescano 1965a: 570). Indeed, following the custom of the Spanish *mesta*, a 1565 ordinance required fences to be taken down after the harvest so that livestock might graze on the remaining stubble, as it did in Spain. In Spain much of the livestock belonged to small landholders who were thereby able to graze their livestock on the land of the large landholders. In Mexico, however, virtually all of the livestock was owned by rich Spaniards, who thus put it to feed on the poor Indians' lands (Chevalier 1970: 57). The aforementioned 1567 ordinance which allowed Indian towns 500 *varas* in all directions and prohibited Spanish cattle ranches within 1000 *varas* of an Indian town afforded the Indians only the most inadequate protection. A later ordinance observed:

The owners of ranches and lands are entering those of the Indians, taking them away and appropriating them, sometimes through violence and other times through fraud, for which reason the miserable Indians leave their homes and their towns, which is what the Spaniards seek and want; they thus arrange it that the 1000 *varas* or 500 *varas* that are supposed to separate them from the towns, are measured from the church or the hermitage which is usually in the centre of the town.   (quoted in Sandoval 1951: 137–8)

That the underlying causes and the immediate drive of this Spanish appropriation of Indian lands were primarily economic and commercial, appears from an analysis of the regional distribution of this land appropriation. Chevalier observes that Spanish appropriation of Indian lands was particularly great in the region covered by the Marquesado del Valle. Since the political organization and control of that region differed some-what from others, Chevalier attributes the difference in land appropriation to the difference in political control:

There appears to have been almost no supervision in the Marqués del Valle's state, even though it contained several of the richest, most densely populated regions in New Spain... Purchases [of land from the Indians] were very heavy, especially in the cane-growing region of Cuernevaca, in Oaxaca, and, sporadically, around Tehuantepec. Legal formalities were flouted to a greater degree than elsewhere, it seems, probably because royal authority was weaker.
(Chevalier 1970: 216)

The reason for this Spanish appropriation of Indian lands is indeed clarified by the facts that Chevalier observes and reports, but the form of administrative control which Chevalier thinks to be determinant is merely circumstantial. It is not, I suggest, that political control was deficient in the Marquesado del Valle (which was incidentally one of the most populated and richest areas of New Spain) but rather the other way around. I suggest that it was primarily the population and wealth of this region, and only incidentally its administrative organization, that accounted for the exceptionally high degree of Spanish appro-priation of Indian lands. That is to say, the Spaniards appropriated Indian lands where these were productive (and for that reason), in or near a centre of high population density which provided a market for what was produced. This inter-pretation of an economic and commercial determinant of land appropriation is further confirmed by Chevalier's own obser-vation that within the Marquesado del Valle the greatest

Spanish appropriation of Indian lands took place in the sugar-producing belt around Cuernavaca (that is its most commercially valuable lands), and secondly in the rich valley of Oaxaca, and only to a lesser degree in the distant and less valuable lands of the Isthmus of Tehuantepec. (This same observation would also seem to disprove Chevalier's hypothesis that the Spanish appropriation of Indian lands was directly related to weak governmental control, since this control is not likely to have been less in Cuernavaca than in distant Tehuantepec, but rather the reverse.) The profitability of sugar growing near Cuernavaca was so great that the Spaniards, as we saw earlier, not only bought and usurped land from the Indians, but even rented it. As a result the production of sugar for the urban and even foreign markets encroached upon the production of maize for Indian consumption in Morelos and other sugar areas, with the notable exception of those near mines, where the high demand for and price of maize and other food staples rendered sugar production relatively less profitable (Moreno Toscano 1965: 41). Moreover, as Chevalier himself points out, exceptionally great Spanish appropriation of Indian land also occurred in Puebla, which is not in the low political control region of the Marquesado del Valle but is another of the richest and most populous regions of New Spain (Chevalier 1970: 138).

It is worth noting that there was resistance to monopoly concentration of landownership in the middle of the sixteenth century in Puebla and towards the end of the century in the Bajio, which had become the agricultural supplier to the northern mines and in part to the capital. However, this successful opposition did not come from the Indians but rather from Spanish and mestizo owners of medium-sized agricultural property. Such successful resistance to monopoly land concentration did not appear in Morelos, where the high capital requirements of the sugar mills gave large capitalists a decided advantage over anybody else. Successful opposition to large capitalists only appeared in the populous region around Puebla, where wheat production could be organized in medium-sized units, and in the Bajio after the mining boom had created analogous conditions there.

Finally, we may ask with Chevalier (1970: 219–20), how much land remained in Indian hands after this Spanish appropriation of the mid sixteenth century. Chevalier says that we do not know. There must have been enough, however, to permit further loss of Indian lands to the growth of the *hacienda* during the last third of the sixteenth century and the seventeenth and eighteenth centuries, and – unless the Indian communities regained some land before and after the turn of the nineteenth century – to leave enough land in Indian hands to allow renewed loss of land after the liberal reforms of 1856.

In summary, during the second period of the colonization of New Spain, that is mainly during the third quarter of the sixteenth century, the progressive incorporation of Mexico's population and agriculture into a single mercantile capitalist economy continued, despite repeated official attempts to create a dual society or economy and to protect the Indian sector thereof. The appropriation and use of land became more and more commercialized and subject to economic and technological determinants emanating from the development of the economy of New Spain as a whole – and indeed of Spain and the mercantilist world. The collection and utilization of Indian tribute, both in the form of labour and in the form of goods and money, came to be organized through new institutions which transformed this tribute into forms of surplus appropriation no longer usually recognized as such. *Encomienda* labour service increasingly gave way to the *repartimiento* forced – but paid – labour draft. *Encomienda* tribute in kind and cash was superseded by *corregimiento* taxes and politically monopolized trade. Agricutural production and distribution among both Spaniards and Indians became more tightly integrated into the expanding new mercantile capitalist market structure. Yet the structure of this market became increasingly monopolistic, so that the benefits that a part of the Indian population derived from it – and therefore its apparent participation in the market – declined. Compared with pre-hispanic times, part of the Indian population was pushed or forced to withdraw into subsistence or below subsistence farming and existence.

Part II

The development of the *hacienda*

4 ✤ 1575-1580: demographic and economic crisis

The third period of colonial rule in Mexico may be said to date from 1575 and to run on well into the seventeenth century. Several transcendental economic events – the economic depression in Spain and Europe, the decline of the Indian population and of mining output in New Spain, the continuing growth of cities – and the responses both by the Spanish and by the Indians to these events in Mexico – viceregal attempts to control monopoly speculation in urban markets by administrative measures, the rise of the *hacienda* and its increasing reliance on *gañán* or 'free' debt bondage labour, and the consolidation of the new Indian community – made this period into one of major importance not only for the colonial era but in the formation of agricultural institutions that have survived into our century. For these reasons, perhaps, this period, and in particular its agricultural history, has received extraordinary attention from historians of Mexico. These students of history have supplied us with a veritable gold mine of secondary sources on the period. Some have also left us their interpretations of these events. One of these interpretations, the thesis of the 'century of depression' (Borah 1951) in which Mexico tended to 'withdraw behind her frontiers' (Chevalier 1970) thereby causing the most important growth and consolidation of the latifundium or *hacienda* in the history of Mexico (Borah

1951, Chevalier 1970, Wolf, 1959), will demand our special attention.

This depression–retrenchment thesis is important not only because it sums up the interpretation of this crucial period by its most knowledgeable students, but because its validity has significance for the whole question of the causes of the growth and survival of the latifundium not only in seventeenth-century Mexico but also in Latin America, and possibly elsewhere, at all times. I shall try to demonstrate in what follows that the historical evidence presented by Chevalier and Borah themselves, if subjected to economic analysis, suggests that the growth of the latifundium in seventeenth-century Mexico was not a depression-induced retrenchment of the economy into what has come to be called a feudal *hacienda*, but that on the contrary the *hacienda* grew and flourished at this time, as at all other times and places in Latin America, because events elsewhere in the national and indeed in the world economy rendered latifundium production highly profitable. Such an analysis of seventeenth-century Mexican agricultural history and interpretation of the growth of the latifundium may then play a key role in our understanding of all Mexican agricultural history, including the rebirth of the latifundium after Mexico's supposedly 'anti-feudal' revolution of 1910; in our analysis of the growth of the latifundium elsewhere in Latin America (such as in sixteenth-century Brazil, seventeenth-century West Indian islands, eighteenth-century Chile, nineteenth-century Argentina, Cuba, Mexico, Brazil) and the contemporary survival and growth of the latifundium everywhere in Latin America and possibly elsewhere; and in our evaluation of the contemporary land reform policies that suppose the *hacienda* to be an outmoded institutional survival without any continuing social function. This analysis of the growth of the latifundium in seventeenth-century Mexico can even help to illuminate the structure and development of the system of world capitalism which permits and indeed requires this latifundium. Finally, a better understanding of this particular case of latifundium growth can not only guide effective land reform policy to eliminate the latifundium but it can also suggest the policy that is necessary to deal with the economic system – national and world capitalism – in which the latifundium and its consequent ills are rooted.

The administration of Viceroy Martin Enriquez de Alanza (1568–80) was marked by the epidemic of 1575–8 and the heavy rains of 1577, which wrought havoc on the population, labour force, and general economic organization in New Spain. The decline in mining production, which was caused in part by reduction in the labour force and in part by the exhaustion of easily accessible surface ores, and the contemporaneous economic depression in Spain and consequent reduction of trade with New Spain added to the dislocation in the existing economic organization to which Viceroy Enriquez, his successors, and their subjects had to adapt. The American historian, Raymond Lee, said of their responses: 'The measures which they adopted were largely determined by conditions peculiar to Mexico' (Lee 1947: 650). Though he is referring specifically to viceregal and municipal short-term attempts to deal with the shortage of grain and other foodstuffs, what Lee says is substantially true also of the remainder of the responses to these economic events. Though the resulting institutions and administrative measures were not peculiar to Mexico (i.e. they existed elsewhere), they did spring up indigenously in Mexico in response to the economic problems that had to be faced there. If similar institutions and measures were found elsewhere, it was because other regions generated similar responses to common problems. What must be emphasized is that these institutions and other responses to seventeenth-century economic problems in Mexico and elsewhere in Latin America did not result simply from the transfer from Spain to New Spain of already existing institutions. Indeed, we have seen that throughout the first half-century of their colonial enterprise, the Spaniards were guided by a vision of a dual economy in which the Spanish and Indian sectors were to remain substantially separate (except, of course, for the exaction of tribute from one sector for the benefit of the other). Their fundamental need to maintain and expand this exploitative relationship between the Spanish and Indian sectors made the hoped-for separation between the sectors increasingly impossible or untenable. In the Spanish response to the population, mining, and other crises following the epidemic of 1575, this vision of a dual economy and the separation of the economy into Spanish and Indian sectors was totally abandoned and replaced by institutions and measures which would *de jure* and *de facto* integrate the two sectors into one single Mexican economy. This Mexican economy, of course, was in turn an integral part of the Spanish empire and of the expanding mercantile capitalist system; and the Mexican Indian, in turn, was fully integrated into this system – in the role of exploited producer that is, not as a consumer of its spoils.

According to Cook and Simpson (Borah 1951: 3) the total population of central Mexico was 4,400,000 in 1565 and 2,500,000 in 1597. According to later estimates by Borah and Cook (1962: 5) the population of central Mexico was 2,650,000 in 1568, 1,900,000 in 1580, and 1,375,000 in 1595. Both sets of estimates reflect a large population decline due to the epidemic of 1575–8 and its aftermath. Both contemporary and modern sources agree that the deaths occurred almost entirely in the Indian population. A contemporary viceregal survey claimed a death toll of two million from the epidemic; Archbishop Pedro Moya de Contreras suggested that one half of the Indian population perished in the epidemic, and another contemporary report said that more than two thirds of the Indian population had died (Lee 1947: 649). Viceroy Martin Enriquez complained that in consequence New Spain suffered from severe labour shortages and that crops were left standing in the fields for lack of workers to harvest them (Chevalier 1970: 64). The quantity demanded did not, however, decline in the same proportions as the quantity supplied. Writing a few years later in 1595 but reflecting also the situation during and immediately after the epidemic, the second Viceroy Velasco reported to the king in Spain:

Since those who consume are many and the Indians who produce are few, supplies have become so short that this year no one has come forward to contract to supply meat, for neither sheep nor cattle are to be found. All supplies are becoming scarce and are rising in price so fast that before many

years this land will experience as great a dearth and want as now exists in
Spain.   (Borah 1951: 23)

Not only did the consuming Spanish population of the city not
decline as much as the producing Indian population of the land,
but it actually increased. The urban population continued to
grow throughout this period, and it was even fed by an
increased influx of immigrants from Spain who were escaping
from the depression-caused decline in economic oportunities
there. Viceroy Velasco also described in the already cited letter.

the need and general shortage which this land is suffering and which is
increasing daily because of the many who come from abroad and the natural
increase among those here, for they have no way to earn a living. It is true
that many are citizens of cities (aside from traders, of whom few are wealthy)
but all others in general are in want.   (Borah 1951: 22)

The increase in demand relative to supply forced up prices,
particularly those of foodstuffs, and made hoarding and speculation more profitable than ever. These in turn increased both
shortages and prices in a vicious output inflationary spiral (the
role of the supply of money in this inflation will be examined
below). Thus in the early 1560s a *fanega* of maize cost two to
three *reales*. Between 1563 and 1566 the price of maize at royal
auctions was increased to five to six *reales* per *fanega*. The rapid
price increase of the 1570s induced by the epidemic and
subsequent shortages was met with attempts at price control.
Lee notes and comments: 'The official maximum prices for 1578,
however, ranged from 10 to 14 *reales*, indicating that they had
risen to much greater heights on the competitive market' (Lee
1947: 658).

Price control and other attempts to administer the market
were not, of course, new in New Spain, or Spain, or Europe.
But with the shortages and market disorganization caused by
the 1575 epidemic, official regulatory measures increased in
number, scope, and depth. Moreover, new measures were
enacted and old measures re-enacted, repeatedly over the next
fifty years, as new measures were needed to deal with new
shortages or as old measures were found to be ineffective (Borah
1951: 24). Lee reviews some of the regulatory measures that
were enacted in 1578 and 1579:

On May 6 1577, the viceroy loaned the cabildo six thousand pesos so that it might purchase wheat at Atlixco, and on September 3 the audiencia enacted legislation requiring the Indians to make their tribute payments to their community treasuries in maize and wheat, rather than in money. Further to stimulate production each tributary Indian was required to farm a plot of land sixty feet square on which one of the two grains was grown.

When these measures failed to halt speculation and rising prices, the audiencia proceeded to enact legislation that fixed the price of maize throughout the colony. By an *auto* of June 3 1578, the retail price of maize in the capital and Veracruz highway areas was pegged at fourteen *reales* per *fanega*...A new law, hastily drafted and proclaimed on November 21 [1578], contained provisions covering the sale of wheat, maize, barley, oats, and rye. Aimed particularly at speculators, it provided that all pre-harvest contracts that had been made with farmers and *encomenderos* for the purchase of their wheat and maize were to be submitted to the *alcalde del crimen*, Hernando de Robles, for examination. Those agreements that involved quantities greater than that necessary for the provisioning of the purchaser and his household were to be invalidated. Bakers were required to furnish a statement of their daily production of bread and excessive amounts of wheat and flour were to be taken from them...[The cabildo] requested that the city be given the royal-tribute maize and wheat of the area for fourteen leagues around Mexico City at the prices secured at the royal auctions of 1575–1576. This request was granted by [Viceroy] Enríquez...Three days later the audiencia extended its controls to include private-tribute maize...Particular provision was made for the Indians of Mexico City...they were guaranteed one-quarter of all the maize distributed by the city.

(Lee 1947: 651, 652, 653, 657)

In 1579 and 1580 the government went still further and created first the *pósito* and then the *alhóndiga*. The *cabildo* and *ayuntamiento* of the city of Mexico (the city council) introduced the statute creating the *pósito* as follows:

That since for the last few years wheat, flour, and maize have been getting each day dearer in this republican city, so that poor and needy Spaniards as well as Indians cannot sustain themselves except by much work...and to remedy this...there should be in this city a *pósito* as there are in many cities in Spain and that it should be wheat, flour, and maize.

(Florescano 1965a: 616)

As Florescano (1965a: 617) explains, the *pósito* was an official agency created to counteract shortages and speculation by buying at officially pegged prices when these were low on the free market, and selling at lower ceiling prices when the free market price was high. To do so, the *pósito* required a large amount of relatively liquid capital of its own, which however it lacked and which could not easily have been provided. To help the city and its *pósito* Viceroy Coruña sold them 13,660 *fanegas* of viceregal tribute maize in 1583 at the below market price of ten *reales* per *fanega*, with the proviso that it be re-sold to the citizens of Mexico at the same price (Lee 1947: 659). Not unlike similar anti-speculative financial institutions in other times and places, the *pósito* of Mexico was never very successful. Its inadequacy led to the establishment of its sister institution, the *alhóndiga*.

The *alhóndiga* was a warehouse which was supplied by obligatory delivery of foodstuffs and which in turn sold these at controlled prices. The central *alhóndiga* was established in the capital, and others were erected elsewhere. Florescano comments:

It is also evident that the municipal administration of Mexico tried, through these twin but not identical institutions, to solve the principal problem that they then faced: provisioning in times of scarcity. The creation of the *alhóndiga* tended to solve the problem of the free and arbitrary sale price, as well as to eliminate the middleman or speculator who raised the prices. At the same time, the storage of all the grain in a particular place, supervised by the municipal authorities, made it possible to keep detailed track of the food needs of the city in each season of the year; this encouraged certain preventive measures and better control was maintained over production, distribution, and the sale of grain.   (Florescano 1965a: 618)

Of the two sister institutions, the *alhóndiga* was by far the more useful. According to Viceroy Enríquez, the creation of the *alhóndiga* was the most effective instrument in preventing fraud and speculation (Lee 1947: 659).

Two other characteristics of the *pósito* and *alhóndiga* are noteworthy for they reflect the distribution of economic and political power in New Spain, and thereby teach us something about the nature of the system as a whole. One is the financing of these institutions. In years of plenty, their stocks were allowed to decline. They had to buy at rising prices therefore during periods of scarcity, and they had to sell at below market prices. Accordingly, although they did thereby dampen the fluctuations in prices and profits, the institutions necessarily operated at a loss that had to be made up from somewhere. Significantly, this loss was made up by royal subsidy, that is at governmental or public expense, and not at the expense of the growers or large merchants (Lee 1947: 659). Secondly, because the operations of the *pósito* were necessarily in competition with the large growers and merchants, these opposed the institution where and when they could. Moreover, perhaps thanks in part to their pressure, the administration of the *pósito* – and particularly the use made of its liquid capital – was not always in practice what it was in theory (Florescano 1965a: 622–3).

5 ❧ Growth of the latifundium: alternative theses

Two further developments in the aftermath of the epidemic of 1576–8 were of still greater importance. One was the decline in mining output, which was caused in part by the exhaustion of easily accessible surface ores and in part by the labour shortage that had been caused by the epidemic. The other was the spread and growth of the *hacienda* and the associated development of *gañán* or debt peon labour as the institutions that were to dominate Mexican agriculture until the post-revolutionary twentieth-century land reform. With this second development – perhaps the most important in the entire history of Mexican agriculture – the original Spanish intent to maintain a dual economy with separate Spanish and Indian sectors was definitely abandoned as a guideline for most of Mexican agriculture. For that reason alone, this period and its institutional developments deserve special attention. Yet the attention that these developments have so far received from historians of the period provides a further reason for a careful review of them here: some of the most important interpretations are, as I hope to show, inconsistent both with the evidence presented in the case of Mexico and with other instances of latifundium growth in the history of Latin America.

What is the origin of the latifundium and what are the reasons for its persistence and growth? Before the studies of the *encomienda* by Zavala (1943 and others) and Miranda (1952, 1965) and the research on the Mexican *hacienda*/latifundium in the late sixteenth and early seventeenth centuries by Chevalier (first published in Paris in 1952) and by Borah (1951), the origin of the *hacienda* or latifundium in Mexico was almost universally attributed to the *encomienda* (Simpson and others). And in many other countries of Latin America, and of course in Europe and North America, this interpretation still persists widely. Whether the *hacienda* is specifically related to the *encomienda* or not, it is almost universally regarded as a feudal institution imported to Latin America by feudal Spaniards from feudal sixteenth century Spain. The persistence of the latifundium into our day in most parts of Latin America is then vaguely explained by reference to the survival of feudal institutions and mentality in a rural hinterland that is substantially isolated from the more progressive, capitalist, outward-looking, industrial and commercial sectors of the economy and society in, especially, the capitals and other major cities. The economic development policy associated with this interpretation of Mexican and Latin American historical and contemporary reality is, of course, primarily that of the removal of these archaic, outdated, feudal institutions, which are regarded as the principal obstacles to development and modernization, and the incorporation of rural regions and their populations into the developing market economy of the cities and of the world. Chevalier's research into the growth of the great latifundia in Mexico and that of Borah on New Spain's (seventeenth) century of depression have definitively shown that the important growth of the *hacienda* in the last third of the sixteenth century and the first two thirds of the seventeenth century was not simply a consequence of the development of the *encomienda*, which moreover was itself already on the decline during the last half of the sixteenth century. The spread and growth of the *hacienda* and the development of *gañán* or debt peon labour as a substitute for the *repartimiento* and earlier *encomienda* labour is shown by these authors to have been the Mexican response to Mexican needs in the seventeenth century, that is the second century of colonization and not the first. We have already seen that the same may be said of the regulations and institutions for the urban distribution of grain, particularly following the epidemic of 1576. In demonstrating then that the growth of the latifundium in Mexico was an indigenous development and not a simple transfer or transplant of institutions from the Old World to the New, Chevalier and Borah achieved an important historical and scientific advance. Nonetheless, as we shall see, their interpretation of this native development leaves the thesis of the feudal *hacienda* essentially intact. Though neither Chevalier nor Borah use the word 'feudal' in their description or analysis of the *hacienda*, others find no difficulty in incorporating this new research and interpretation into the old thesis of feudal Mexico and Latin America.

According to Chevalier and Borah the Mexican *hacienda* grew and strengthened because the Mexican economy turned in upon itself during a depression which obliged the population to retreat on to the land and into the *hacienda*. Woodrow Borah begins his essay 'New Spains Century of Depression' thus:

In this paper I shall interpret the movement of Mexican colonial economy in terms of demographic findings. I shall indicate that from 1576 until well over a century later New Spain had a contracting economy. Further, this long period of depression was a major factor in molding the Mexican land and labor systems which became deominant in the seventeenth century and remained so to the Revolution of 1910. My interpretation is obviously a hypothesis which needs much additional investigation.'

Borah concludes the same study:

If this hypothesis is sound, the precipitate and sustained decrease in the Indian hewers of wood and drawers of water after the demographic plateau of 1546–1576, the years when the white upper stratum became firmly established in the colony, confronted the new dominant group with one of the most severe and difficult problems of the colonial period. The problem was made more difficult by the fact that the Spanish actually increased steadily as the Indians diminished. The efforts of the Spanish to solve the problem, to continue to draw products and services in accustomed volume from the Indian under-strata, speeded up and perhaps led directly to a radical reorganization of land holding and labor forms which greatly extended and strengthened the emerging hybrid Mexican culture. At the end of the seventeenth century, the distinctively Mexican economy was already organized on the basis of latifundia and debt peonage, the twin aspects of Mexican life which continued nearly to our day and which helped provoke the revolution of 1910–1917
(Borah 1951: 1, 44)

In his later study written with Sherburne Cook, 'La despoblación del México Central en el siglo XVI' (1962), Borah returns to the same thesis.

Though he does not use the word 'depression', François Chevalier goes still further in his interpretation, which attributes the growth and consolidation of the *hacienda* in the seventeenth century to commercial decline:

Thus New Spain showed a tendency to withdraw behind her frontiers when silver production fell off to practically nothing in the early eighteenth century...The tendency to what amounted in fact to decentralization is one of the aspects of the general recession which accompanied the decline of the mines in the seventeenth century, the relative shrinkage of commerce, and the isolation of the entire country...This return to the land, associated with impoverishment and a partially closed economy, is one aspect of the general recession affecting the Spanish Indies in the seventeenth century...haciendas were tending to become little self-contained worlds, whereas they had been created largely to produce food and beasts for the great mines...The return to the soil helped revive in Mexico certain medieval institutions and customs recalling the patriarchal existence of Biblical times...In the early decades of the seventeenth century the silver boom collapsed, smothering in its passage the first stirrings of a barely nascent capitalism. The land became the sole source of income.   (Chevalier 1970: 41, 48, 66, 180, 307, 309)

Other scholars appear to have accepted this interpretation unquestioningly. Eric Wolf, for instance, writes:

But the depression of the seventeenth century put an end to utopian dreaming...Middle America again retreated into its countryside...Offspring of an economic depression, the hacienda was set up to feed a limited demand. With its external markets dried up by an economic downturn and by political weakness in the mother country, it relied on markets within the colony.
(Wolf 1959: 202, 204)

(Gibson does not deal at all with the question of what caused the growth of the *hacienda*.)

Beyond the question of its consistency with historical facts, to which I shall turn below, this interpretation raises a number of serious difficulties. Firstly, all of the authors cited above agree that prior to the period under discussion the *hacienda* grew in Mexico in response to increased demand for its products or was stimulated by technological or social conditions that made its growth profitable. The initial development and growth of the *hacienda*, it is clear, was to produce wheat and meat as well as hides and other products for the growing cities of central Mexico and the rising demand of the expanding northern mines. Why then should the especially large growth of the latifundium and its 'consolidation' in the period after 1576 be attributed, not to a continued and accelerated growth in the demand for its products and/or to other sources of its profitability, but rather the opposite – that is, to a depression-associated decline in demand and economic retrenchment? If originally the *hacienda* was 'organized for commercial ends' (Wolf 1959: 204), if it was a capitalist enterprise, as Wolf (1959: 204) and Bazant (1950) have called it, if it had grown up to supply 'the large and expanding market of the Spanish cities' (Borah 1951: 32), and if there are abundant examples of 'silver mining's close link with the great rural haciendas' rise and expansion in the north' (Chevalier 1970: 167), why should we suppose that the birth of new and the expansion of old *haciendas* in the period after 1576 contributed to the birth of typically medieval institutions with which all of the fever of a nascent capitalism disappeared? This paradox evidently bears further examination. The paradox disappears however, as I hope to show, if we re-examine the evidence for the later period of *hacienda* growth.

Another difficulty in interpreting the growth of the latifundium in seventeenth-century Mexico as the result of an economic depression whose reduction in demand led to retrenchment into the *hacienda* is that this interpretation of the growth of the *hacienda* is inconsistent with clear evidence of demand and profitability-induced latifundium growth at other times and/or places in the history of Latin America. Chevalier himself says that the golden age of the Mexican *hacienda* was in the eighteenth century, that is, during a period of renewed increase in mining output and demand for agricultural commodities (Chevalier 1970: 263, 311). Beyond that, as one can see from an examination of the Porfiriato, the spectacular growth of the latifundium and of the associated debt peonage labour in Mexico in the last third of the nineteenth century is unmistakably associated with the accelerated growth of demand, in part from the United States, for the agricultural products of the Mexican land. Indeed, the rebirth of the Mexican latifundium in our day, after the post-revolutionary land reform, is also demand-induced and can hardly be attributed to the survival and much less to the rebirth of a depressed or feudal economy, especially in the northern states of Mexico. Similarly, the growth of the sugar-producing latifundia of the Caribbean in the seventeenth and eighteenth centuries (and notably those of Cuba in the nineteenth and twentieth centuries) and the growth of the wheat and livestock latifundia of Argentina and Uruguay in the nineteenth century, cannot be attributed either to the transplantation of 'feudal' institutions from Europe three centuries earlier or to a depression-induced retrenchment at that time. Instead, in all these cases (that is, in most instances in Latin America), the growth of the latifundium was clearly caused by and must be attributed to the increase in its profitability, due to the increase in demand for its products or to technologically created cost reductions (such as the railroad or shipping). It has recently been established conclusively that the growth of the latifundium in eighteenth-century Chile and the spread of *inquilino* or peon labour there, was also due to an increase in the demand for agricultural products, in this case as a result of the opening of a market for Chilean wheat in Lima and later elsewhere in the world (Góngora 1960, Borde and Góngora 1956, Sepúlveda 1959, Baraona *et al.*, and Frank 1967, 1969). Though it may not accord with widespread notions about the feudal nature of the latifundium, the evidence is clear that the normal growth of the latifundium in Latin America is profit-induced. Though this does not disprove the Chevalier–Borah thesis it evidently casts further doubt upon it.

The Chevalier–Borah thesis of depression-induced latifundium growth is also inconsistent, at least in part, with a view of the general structure and development of the Latin American economy as a fully integral commercial part of the world mercantile capitalist and later of the industrial capitalist system, as it is increasingly analysed by such authors as Bagú, Furtado, Simonsen, Prado Junior, Vitale, Arcila Farías, Florescano, Wolf (1959), Frank (1967 and elsewhere). This interpretation certainly admits of the existence of a relatively non-commercial and isolated *hacienda*, but not of the growth of the *hacienda* or latifundium under the circumstances and with the characteristics identified by Chevalier and Borah.

6 ❧ 1580-1630: profit-generated latifundium growth

The three principal causes to which Borah and Chevalier attribute the seventeenth-century depression-caused growth of the latifundium in Mexico are the decline in the population, the decline in mining output, and the depression in Spain with its consequent decrease in commercial intercourse between Spain and New Spain. These three historical events did indeed take place; but, upon closer examination, they did not produce in Mexico, and least of all in its agricultural sector, any of the characteristics which we would today attribute to an economic depression and especially to an agricultural depression. Far from having reduced the relative or even the absolute profitability of large-scale latifundium agriculture, these three historical events (and other factors) appear to have increased agricultural demand and profitability for Spanish *hacienda* producers.

The decline in population after the epidemic of 1576 was undeniably great. As noted above, Cook and Simpson (1948, cited in Borah 1951: 3) estimated that there was a decline in central Mexico from 4,400,000 in 1565 to 2,000,000 in 1607 and to 1,500,000 in 1650. (Borah and Cook (1962: 5) estimate 2,640,000 for 1568 and 1,075,000 for 1605). The result was a permanent deficit in the labour supply (Lee 1947: 649). Borah suggests that 'we may guess that the economic contraction was nearly, though not quite equal, to the decline in Indian numbers' (Borah 1951: 4). Yet Borah himself emphasizes that while the Indian population declined, the white population grew (Borah 1951: 18, 20, 25). Cook and Simpson estimate that the so-called white population of central Mexico grew from 57,000 in 1570 to 114,000 in 1646 (or 63,000 to 125,000 for New Spain

51

as a whole) (Borah 1951: 3). Indeed, Borah points out on the same page that 'the figures in Table I indicate beyond question that contraction must have taken place at least in the Indian economy of central Mexico as distinct from the economy associated with the European conquerers'. Moreover Borah goes on to emphasize that

The Spanish towns of New Spain not only survived this long period of economic contraction but unlike the mother country also gained strength during it as is evident from their steady, if slow increase in population from 1570 to 1646 and their rapid increase in the century following. Their survival, and even quasi-prosperity, resulted not from grim endurance but rather from the success of at least some of the measures they took to meet the major problems of service and production.   (Borah 1951: 30)

Chevalier is also aware of this increase in the non-Indian population, for he notes that at the end of the sixteenth-century New Spain had perhaps 100,000 white inhabitants whereas a century later it had 200,000 whites plus 50,000 *mestizos* and 50,000 Negroes and mulattos (Chevalier 1970: 41). The population decline, then, did not mean the unmitigated and general contraction of economic activity and particularly of demand that we associated with depression but did permit, if not provide for, an increase in the number of urban consumers of agricultural commodities. This does not yet establish that there was an increase in demand for agricultural commodities produced by the *hacienda*, but at least it does not preclude it, as is implied by the depression thesis.

The decline in New Spain's mining output during this period is now also beyond dispute. Chevalier places this decline first in Zacatecas, then in San Luis Potosí, and after 1620–30 everywhere in New Spain (Chevalier 1970: 179). Borah (1951: 33) places the peak of mining output in the last decade of the sixteenth century. From then on output declined slowly until 1630 and after that rapidly until 1660. Only then did output again begin to rise to attain by about 1690 the earlier level of production of the 1580s. In his 1953 review of Chevalier's thesis Pierre Chaunu says, however:

François Chevalier thinks that it is necessary to place the maximum vigour of the latifundium in this period of contraction...It seems difficult to maintain that this correlation is as simple as François Chevalier thinks. Our own work suggests that we should move the reversal in the principal trend over some twenty years in the economic space of the Spanish empire. We would, in fact, draw a curve which would break around 1620 and not in 1595 and which would correspond better, we think at least, to the general curve of prices in the Spanish world.   (Chaunu 1956: 280, 281)

If Chaunu is correct, the first half-century of 'depression' would no longer support Chevalier's and Borah's interpretation of the growth of the *hacienda* during this period. Instead, it would strengthen still further the case made below for demand-induced *hacienda* growth.

Whatever its precise timing, the decline in mining output in New Spain has been attributed primarily to the exhaustion of the surface deposits, which were easier to reach at less cost, and to the attendant increase in the cost of mining. Secondary causes have been found in the increase in taxes on mine profits that the crown imposed because of its own financial distress, as well as the increase in the price of and taxes on quicksilver, which the mine owners needed to reduce their ores. Borah suggests an additional reason: 'The chief product, silver, brought a fixed return of approximately one peso an ounce at the same time that prices were rising for labor, food, fodder, and for most of the supplies the mines had to use' (Borah 1951: 43). Herein, of course, Borah contradicts his depression thesis, at least as far as the prices and presumable profitability of food and other agricultural products is concerned. But that is a matter to be considered below. For now, let us emphasize the importance of another part of this statement. Borah tells us quite clearly that the profitability of mining decreased, because the costs of mining increased while the monetary value per unit output – he calls it return – remained fixed. That would be reason enough to discourage investment in mines, to reduce their production and to transfer capital from mining to a sector in which prices were rising at that time – agriculture, as Borah himself tells us. Indeed, Chevalier (1970: 165–84) reports numerous cases of mine owners who first acquired land and built *haciendas* as part of their total enterprises and then devoted themselves increasingly to farming and commerce to the exclusion of mining. Chevalier says that we do not know the extent of this transfer.

Whatever the extent may have been, the important question for Chevalier and for us is the reason for this transfer. Did the mine owners, merchants, and other capitalists take their capital into the *hacienda* in order to retreat into a closed, isolated economy that was turning in upon itself? Or did they withdraw their capital from mining and other sectors to invest it in the growing latifundia because the profitability of mining was decreasing both absolutely and relatively to the profitability of large-scale farming? Borah had already supplied part of the answer in the sentence quoted above. However, it may be suggested that the profitability of mining did not just decrease absolutely because costs increased and returns remained the same. Much of this period, as we observed in the discussion of the grain crisis of 1580 and as we shall see in our examination of prices below, was marked by inflation in New Spain. Did not, then, fixed prices for silver mean a falling return, even if costs had remained fixed as well? To say that in a period of inflation the prices of goods and services increased is to say, in other words, that the value or the price of money decreased. And was it not money that the mine owners were producing in their mines since the price of silver was fixed? The implication is that they faced both an increase in costs *and* a decrease in returns – enough reason for any capitalist to reduce his output and put his money into some other business, if possible. Yet, at this very time, as will be argued below, the profitability of latifundium agriculture was rising. Faced then with declining profits in mining and rising profits in large-scale agriculture, any rational capitalist would surely withdraw his capital from mining and invest it in agriculture to the greatest extent possible; and if he was already operating in both sectors, as well as in commerce, as many sixteenth- and seventeenth-century capitalists in Mexico were, this transfer would be all the easier and more normal. To explain it, we would have no need of a hypothesis of depression or retrenchment, reliance on which raises the difficulties of scientific consistency noted earlier.

The third cause of the supposed depression in New Spain

was the depression in Spain itself: 'after 1575 Spain herself entered upon an economic and demographic decline that was not arrested until the beginning of the eighteenth century. The mother country's loss of economic strength meant additional difficulties for her colonies' (Borah 1951: 29). The relation of Spain's depression to its commercial contact with its colonies has been documented by Albert Payson Usher through his account of the movement of ships (cited in Larraz López 1943: 81). The tonnage of shipping from the New World to Spain, which around 1600 was 21,000 tons, dropped to about 10,000 tons for the period 1640–50, and 5,600 tons for 1670–80. Following Haring and Hamilton, Chevalier also notes that towards the end of the seventeenth century shipping to New Spain was only a quarter of what it had been about a century earlier. It is not clear, however, why this reduction of contact between Spain and its colonies, and particularly the decline in Spain's export of its manufactured goods to its colonies, should have contributed to a general depression in the colonies. On the contrary, at least as far as the manufacturing sector is concerned, Spain's loss could have been expected to have been its colonies' gain. And indeed so it was. Throughout its empire, including New Spain, the depression in Spain led to a growth of manufacturing industries in the colonies both for their own consumption and for export. (For an analysis of this pheno- menon and a review of industrial development in Latin America during times of depression and war in the metropolis, see Frank 1967, and the chapter 'The development of underdevelopment' in Frank 1969.) This spurt of manufacturing in New Spain and elsewhere, particularly in the textile industries, presumably created a demand for agricultural raw materials to be processed. At the same time, as Borah notes (1951: 29), the depression- induced decline in economic opportunities in Spain increased the emigration of Spaniards to the colonies, including New Spain, where they settled in large part in the cities and added to some extent to the urban consumer demand of non-productive Spaniards. This explains, of course, part of the increase in the white population during this period, reference to which by Viceroy Velasco has been quoted above and which is also recorded by Borah. Finally, the Spanish depression and other financial pressures led the crown to impose ever higher taxes on its subjects, including those in New Spain (Larraz López 1943: 79). To some extent, these taxes fell more highly on mine owners than on landowners. To the extent that they fell on land, they also encouraged the formation and expansion of latifundia, as we shall see below, by promising legal title to illegally obtained land upon the payment of a legalization fee to the exchequer.

Up to this point, then, our examination of the historical evidence surrounding the three causes of the supposed seventeenth century depression in New Spain and the associated retrenchment into an agriculture that turned in upon itself in isolation from the remainder of the economy – that is, the decline in population, decline in mining output, and depression in Spain – supports neither the thesis of a generalized depression in New Spain nor the interpretation of economic contraction as the cause of the growth of the latifundium. We may now proceed to examine the evidence of the growth of the latifundium itself and the development of debt tied *gañán* labour, in order to seek the real causes for this institutional development and its perpetuation.

'Hacienda, perhaps more than any other single colonial topic, still needs systematic investigation, not alone in the Valley of Mexico but in all areas', according to Charles Gibson, author of the authoritative study of the Valley of Mexico, *The Aztecs under Spanish Rule* (Gibson 1964: 406). Nonetheless, thanks to Gibson's own work, and to that of Chevalier and Borah as well as others, it is possible to advance the following thesis about the *hacienda*: the *hacienda* grew primarily in response to its profitability, which in turn was a function of increased demand and price for its products and decreased supply from alternative sources. These causes of the growth of the latifundium were particularly conspicuous in the north, where the expansion of mining generated the birth of *haciendas* that produced wheat, livestock, and later maize and other products as well. The acquisition and monopolization of land by the *hacienda* was spurred on by its profitability and was, as it has always been since, particularly conspicuous in the areas where the proximity of cities, roads, or other factors rendered land particularly valuable. The *hacienda* was a commercial institution from the beginning; and it displayed the same characteristics of mono- polization and speculation that similar commercial institutions have displayed in other sectors of the capitalist market then and now. The productive requirements of this profit-seeking commercial institution called into being new productive rela- tions, *gañán* or debt peon labour, which came to replace the previous institutions of the *encomienda* and *repartimiento* and increasingly to dominate the mode of production in the Mexican countryside.

Before examining the evidence in support of these hypotheses in greater detail, it may be useful to quote the summary statements on this problem by a Mexican historian, whose research appears to be leading him to conclusions very similar to the ones presented here. Enrique Florescano writes:

the decline in the Indian population favoured the development of European agriculture by provoking a decline in agricultural production and thereby a shortage of foodstuffs (maize, beans, etc.). This is because on the one hand the population decline to a certain extent eliminated the competition of cheap supply that was offered by the Indians and on the other hand because the decline in the native population left much land at the disposal of the Spaniards...Finally, we observe in all this that the decade of the 1570s, despite the decline in the native population and the rise in prices, or rather thanks to them, stimulated the development of a commercial type Spanish agriculture, which of course, although administered by Spaniards, continued to rest upon indigenous labour (Florescano 1965a: 600–2)

Florescano continues elsewhere:

We here wish to highlight the causes which motivated the rapid development of agriculture in the above-mentioned regions, in order to compare them with the agricultural situation obtaining in Veracruz. The first thing that stands out as a powerful incentive to the increase in grain agriculture is the foundation of numerous towns and cities in the first decades of the colony and later. There is no doubt that the founding of small and large cities (which in turn developed a monetary and commercial economy) exercised a determining influence on the increase in agricultural production. In fact, the continuing demand of these two centres, as well as the municipal grain legislation that soon appeared, favoured the formation of an ever wider and stable market, which assured the purchase of agricultural products at a good price. The case of Mexico City, the largest consumer centre in New Spain, is highly illuminating in this respect. It is curious how the population growth of Mexico City was proportional to the agricultural development of its surroundings. Thus, as its population increased, in the neighbourhood of the great city there grew up and multiplied a great number of farms and haciendas specializing in the production of grain, which like an immense belt circumscribed the city and took care of its provisions...The main rival of the valleys of Mexico–Toluca in the production of grain was the valley of Puebla–Tlaxcala, whose agricultural development may be explained as in the previous case, by its proximity to the large consumer centres (Puebla, Mexico and the port of Veracruz), and also because of the availability of abundant labour. The rapid development of the production of wheat and maize, which was also observed in this zone...was largely due to the strategic position it occupied. Situated half way between Mexico City and the port of Veracruz, the wheat and maize that was produced in this zone had their sale practically assured especially through the port. We have already seen that the provision of wheat to the port came from Atlixco and Tehuacan. But in addition, as far as we know, this was the only region to export grain abroad...another factor that simulated grain agriculture was the discovery of the mines in the north of New Spain. With the mines came the establishment of the *reales mineros*, and of the ports on 'the frontier of the barbarous Indians'. The migration of a large population towards this region and its distance from the large centres of production were incentives which made it necessary to develop, near the *reales mineros* and the forts, ranches and haciendas to assure provisions for men and beasts as well as to provide the continued labour for the mines...Finally the agriculture that we have been summarizing distinguished itself by a very peculiar characteristic: its markedly commercial character. As distinct from the subsistence agriculture that was common in the regions of Chiapas, Oaxaca, Yucatan, and even in Veracruz, the agriculture of the valleys of Mexico and Puebla or that of the north of New Spain, was an agriculture that produced for the market, be it for that of the large cities (such as Mexico or Puebla), or of the ports (Veracruz, Campeche, Havana, Maracaibo), or of the mining centres (Zacatecas, Guanajuato, Pachuca). These are, then, in general outline, the essential elements that contributed to the development of grain agriculture in the centre and north of the country.

(Florescano 1965b: 73–5)

Having independently come to the same conclusion (Frank 1969: chapter 15), I can only second what Florescano says, and I am moved to suggest that the extent and degree of commercial agriculture was even greater than he suggests. For instance, as noted above, Spanish agriculture in the valley of Oaxaca was certainly commercial in large parts. At the same time, since the production of cochineal by the indigenous population of Oaxaca came to provide New Spain's most important source of foreign exchange after silver, a significant part of the supposedly subsistence agriculture of these Indians was also commercial.

The demand-generated growth of commercial wheat and livestock *haciendas*, to which Florescano refers, was already evident in the second period of the Spanish colonization of Mexico, from 1550 to 1575, as was discussed above. The epidemic of 1576 resulted in a drastic decline of the Indian population and an accompanying disorganization of the productive and distributive section of the economy. As we saw in the discussion of the urban market above, the prices of foodstuffs rose rapidly in the major centres of Spanish population and also in mining areas, working for the benefit of the Spanish economy. As we saw above, the second Viceroy Valesco wrote in 1595 that 'All supplies are becoming scarce and are rising in price so fast' (cited in Borah 1951: 23). The shortages may be traced to the failure of two kinds of suppliers to meet the demand: the Indian communities and the existing Spanish *haciendas*. The small-scale producers in the Indian communities had previously supplied not only the subsistence consumption and local market demand of these communities themselves, but also part of the demand of the urban Spaniards and their Indian and Negro employees and slaves. With the drastic population decline after the epidemic and its consequent disruption of communal life, the supply of agricultural commodities from this communal Indian source was no longer adequate. Secondly, the Spanish *haciendas*, especially those dependent on *repartimiento* Indian labour whose availability also dwindled, were no longer able to meet the commercial demand of the consumers in the urban and mining centres. The urban population, as we saw above, continued to rise throughout this period; and the mining output and demand of the mining centres continued its expansion until at least the 1590s or, as Chaunu would have it, another two decades later.

From the point of view of the colonial authorities, if they viewed the economy as a whole, the existing productive and distributive institutions were no longer adequate to satisfy even the minimum requirements of the Spanish let alone the Indian population. We saw above how they sought to meet the new problems of distribution. The viceregal authorities also turned their attention to the problem of production, in part leading, in part accompanying or following the private development of a dominant new productive institution, the *hacienda*, and the associated debt labour which were to replace the *encomienda* and *repartimiento* (Borah 1951: 32).

From the point of view of individual Spanish entrepreneurs, the social necessity of the economy as a whole opened up private opportunities for them. On the one hand the prices of agricultural products and profitability of large-scale agricultural production increased, and on the other hand population decline weakened and increasingly eliminated the source of competitive supply of agricultural commodities from small-scale Indian communal producers (Borah 1951: 32). Furthermore, the 'social interest' of the society as a whole as seen by the colonial authority now coincided increasingly with the private interests of Spanish entrepreneurs, who sought to exercise their influence over the government to gain increasing protection and favours. Thus, as we shall see below, the lands that were vacated by Indian population decline were increasingly assigned to and sold to Spanish *latifundistas*, or else their illegal or semi-legal use of these lands was confirmed by legal title. Increasingly, Spanish *latifundistas* also managed to make use of the public authority to obtain lands that were still owned and occupied by Indians. Simultaneously, the authorities facilitated the increase of debt peonage. The opportunities created by rising prices of agricultural commodities, and by inflation generally, led then as they always have since to speculation in land and land titles. Land grants were bought and sold and *haciendas* that were built through grants and purchase of land either grew through further purchase or other acquisition of land, or they declined again through the sale of all or part of their land to other *haciendas* (Gibson 1964: 289). The increase in land prices was greatest, of course, near the cities and mines; and that is also where first speculation in land and then the concentration of land into a few hands was most common (Chevalier 1970: 138).

7 ❧ Commercial crop and livestock production

The initial expansion of the Spanish *hacienda* during this period was still primarily for the production of wheat. Irrigated lands especially were turned to the production of wheat, obliging maize farmers to retreat to the less productive non-irrigated hillsides and other lands (Moreno Toscano 1965: 643). The size of the wheat farms increased considerably, and the share of wheat produced by the large farms increased even more. The data collected by Gibson for areas that may or may not be typical show farms planting from zero to eighty-seven *fanegas* of wheat to account for 94% and farms planting over one hundred *fanegas* to account for 6% of that crop's production in 1563 (one sown *fanega* was equivalent to about one and a half acres). By 1602, farms planting in excess of one hundred *fanegas* accounted for 92% of the wheat planted in Tepozotlán (Gibson 1964: 323–5). The market-stimulated production of wheat on large farms continued in the Mexico–Puebla area and spread to the Bajío area, between Mexico City and the northern mines, which was to become the bread-basket of Mexico, though according to Chevalier (1970: 292) the market for wheat declined in other regions. Borah (1951: 25) notes a decline in wheat production in the valley of Atlixco (near Puebla) prior to the year 1631. That this was probably a temporary decline may be surmised from the fact that the years 1631–2 were years of particular crisis, associated both with bad crops and with the special demand for labour created by the crash programme to finish the drainage works on the lake in the Valley of Mexico. Borah also notes some declines in tithes in the mining areas of the north, which he associated with declining supplies of

61

foodstuffs there, possibly due to the decline in mining activity (Borah 1951: 25).

Increasingly, the Spanish *hacienda* became a producer of maize as well as wheat. During the first and second periods of the colonial era maize both for home consumption and for the market had been grown by small-scale producers in the Indian communities. After the epidemic of 1576, the independent small-scale Indian producers to some extent retreated from and to some extent were forced out of the market for maize. By 1630, commercial maize production had passed into Spanish hands. Gibson comments:

In 1630 Indian maize agriculture had been reduced to the status of local subsistence and the city was being supplied by 'wealthy Spaniards'. By this date the hacienda as a maize producer had every advantage over the Indian community. It possessed lands for extensive production and facilities for storage and transportation already developed for wheat. The hacendados controlled Indian labor. They could profitably undersell small producers in bulk transactions or hoard supplies for a seller's market.

(Gibson 1964: 326)

At the same time the production of other staples, such as beans and *maguey* for the extraction of the alcoholic *pulque*, also fell increasingly into *hacienda* hands. As it did, *hacienda* production of wheat became less important since its consumption continued to be confined largely to the white population, while the staples were of course consumed by everybody (Chevalier 1970: 292). In other words, not only the expansion of the *haciendas* but also the productive activity that these undertook responded to the exigencies of the market.

Livestock raising was another important commercial activity of the *hacienda*. Indeed, it may be said to have seen its origin in New Spain as early as the first and second periods of colonial rule (Matesánz 1965: 538). Chevalier emphasizes the commercial characteristics of livestock ranching: 'The estancia economy ...was one that faced outward, dependent as it was on mines that were sometimes far away, on weavers concentrated around Mexico City and Puebla, on Europe, finally, which was a large consumer of American hides.' (Chevalier 1970: 108). The fleet of 1587 carried a hundred thousand hides to Spain, of which 74,350 came from Mexico (Chevalier 1970: 107). Much of the demand, however, was domestic and came from the mines, which used hides for bags to carry ore, water, and so on. Given the periodicity of the fleet and the swings of mining production, the demand for and price of hides and livestock were volatile (Chevalier 1970: 108). This was also the case for sheep, though less so, because the wool they produced went to supply Mexican textile manufacturers whose output was more stable (Chevalier 1970: 108). As we noted earlier, after the original raising of pigs, sheep farming was the first type of important livestock production to expand. It was soon replaced by cattle farming, which dominated during the mid sixteenth century. Beginning with the seventeenth century, sheep raising came increasingly to replace cattle production again. Apart from the decline of cattle herds towards the end of the sixteenth century for biological reasons, the reasons for the shift in livestock production were essentially economic. The first was that the decline in mining production decreased the demand for hides. The second was that the depression in Spain decreased Spanish exports of textiles to the colonies and led to an increase in textile production in New Spain, both for the home market and for export to other parts of Latin America (Chevalier 1970: 291). Indeed, even within New Spain there was a shift towards the use of wool in partial replacement of cotton as the decline in the Indian population reduced the supply of cotton from the low-lying coastal regions and possibly as the population migration into colder regions increased the demand for wool.

The planting of sugar on a large scale also increased again at this time. The colonial authorities, as we noted earlier, had sought to discourage the production of sugar, which was interfering with that of more essential staples. In 1599 the allotment of *repartimiento* Indians to sugar plantations was abolished so that they might be reallocated to the production of wheat. But by that time the sugar plantations had largely ceased to be dependent on *repartimiento* labour and filled their labour requirements more and more through slave labour and, to a larger extent, through wage labour. They also became increasingly autonomous by organizing their own production of livestock for beasts of burden and meat for their workers and the production of other agricultural commodities to supply their food, fuel and clothing needs (Chevalier 1970: 81–2). Though sugar planting had initially been limited to the Veracruz, Puebla, and Morelos regions, it now spread to Guadalajara and Nueva Galicia. By 1618, Mexican sugar production for export was again on the upswing (Moreno Toscano 1965: 646). All this was despite prohibitions against new sugar mills issued in 1601 and increasing complaints by Indians against the usurpation of their maize and other lands by the expansion of sugar (Sandoval 1951: 134–7).

This demand-generated growth of commercial agriculture organized through the *hacienda* is perhaps most conspicuous in the northern mining areas. Humboldt noted this when he wrote at the end of the colonial period:

Were it not for the establishments formed for the working of the mines, how many places would have remained desert? how many districts uncultivated in the four intendancies of Guanaxuato, Zacatecas, San Luis Potosi, and Durango...Farms are established in the neighbourhood of the mine. The high price of provision, from the competition of the purchasers, indemnifies the cultivator for the privations to which he is exposed from the hard life of the mountains. Thus from the hope of gain alone...a mine...becomes in a short time connected with the lands which have long been under cultivation.   (Humboldt 1966: ii, 407–8)

Chevalier makes the same observation (1970: 166 and elsewhere). Mendizábal describes this process in detail in several of his works, especially that on the conquest and colonization and the history of Zacatecas (Mendizábal 1945–6: v). Chevalier comments:

Some of the characteristics already observed in the colonization of the center and south are brought into prominence [in the north], notably the part played by powerful individuals...Not small settlers, but big capitalists and men with independent incomes colonized its reaches: Guadalajara judges and officials in the southwest; rich miners, soldiers, and governors north of Zacatecaz, Guanajuato, and San Luis; merchants, stockmen, and royal officials from Mexico City, in New León, which was occupied later.
                                 (Chevalier 1970: 150)

Mendizábal notes:

Nothing can give us a better idea of the formation of large property in Zacatecas than the latifundios of Colonel Sir Fernando de Campa, first Count of San Mateo de Valparaiso, if we are forewarned that, while the Count was temporarily a fortunate miner, most of his life was devoted to agriculture, livestock, and foresting activities.   (Mendizábal, 1945–6: v, 204)

Eric Wolf summarizes:

The northward expansion was the work of great capitalists, grown rich in mining, stock-raising, and commercial agriculture, not of subsistence farmers, patiently staking a claim for themselves and for their families, as on the later western frontier of North America. When mining output and revenues declined at the end of the sixteenth century, the advance was maintained by stock-breeders, looking for new pastures to feed their enormous herds. Stock-breeding, not cultivation, thus provided the 'cutting edge' of the northward Spanish advance. (Wolf 1959: 194)

In the coastal zones of the gulf and the Pacific, the *hacienda* was still incipient at this time and did not develop until later (Chevalier 1970: 279–80).

In contrast to this picture of the continued demand-generated expansion of large-scale agricultural production organized through the *hacienda*, Chevalier presents a picture which is at once more detailed and more ambiguous, but which in general conveys the impression of an agricultural contraction such as that suggested by Borah's choice of the word 'depression' for the state of the economy as a whole, including agriculture. Chevalier says:

While the great estate was taking on its final form – the hacienda – the mines had become half-deserted, trade had come virtually to a halt, the Spanish merchant fleet had dwindled and its sailings had grown erratic, royal authority seemed to have become more remote, and the country had been withdrawing further and further into isolation... With the exception of a few years when shortages created some inflation, food prices in the seventeenth century, as a matter of fact, leveled off and even dropped... harvests were hard to dispose of, and maize, wheat, and even sugar had little value outside a few favored zones. (Chevalier 1970: 150, 310, 292, 311)

In support of this interpretation, Chevalier gives a few isolated prices of agricultural commodities in a footnote (1952: 382); but it is far from clear that the prices he quotes indicate the general price stability and even decline to which he refers. Borah himself thinks that the evidence is unclear. On the other hand, at one point Chevalier attributes the supposed stability of prices in the seventeenth century to the price regulation of the *pósito* and *alhóndiga* (Chevalier 1970: 65). Furthermore, as we saw, Chevalier sets aside the 'favored zones' when discussing poor prices for producers (Chevalier 1970: 311). He speaks of the 'danger of overproduction' in some areas, among which he includes the Bajío which then supplied the northern mines; but he points out that this does not apply to the regions which supplied Mexico City. As for the prices of livestock and wheat, Chevalier says that they continued to rise from eight or nine *maravedís* for an *arrelde* of beef in 1575 to twenty *maravedís* some time in the early seventeenth century and then to level off at about seventeen *maravedís* after 1622 (Chevalier 1970: 104). With the closing down of the mines in the north, Chevalier says that some of the population returned to the south while others remained on the neighbouring *haciendas* which were 'tending to become little self-contained worlds' (Chevalier 1970: 180). Humboldt had already commented upon this phenomenon:

Moreover, this influence of the mines on the progressive cultivation of the country is more durable than they are themselves. When the seams are exhausted, and the subterraneous operations are abandoned, the population of the canton undoubtedly diminishes, because the miners emigrate elsewhere; but the colonist is retained by his attachment for the spot where he received his birth, and which his fathers cultivated with their hands. The more lonely the cottage is, the more it has charms for the inhabitants of the mountains.
(Humboldt 1966: 408)

But Humboldt is here talking primarily about individual or communal farmers who, with the disappearance of their source of cash earnings, retreat into a community of substantially subsistence production and consumption. Even Chevalier is hardly talking about the *growth* of the *hacienda*. Indeed, in the same passage as that quoted above, he notes that some *haciendas* were abandoned entirely (Chevalier 1970: 180).

Mendizábal emphasizes the problems (which persist to our day) that were created by the abandonment in many regions of central Mexico of populations that were originally attracted by the mines and the associated profitability of agriculture and which remained there to sustain themselves on often very poor land on which agricultural production was profitable only while prices were maintained at a high level through mining demand (Mendizábal 1945–6: II, 493).

8 ✤ The monopolization of land

The formation and expansion of the *hacienda* can also be examined through its accumulation or, better, monopolization of land. When acquiring land, *hacienda* owners were also careful to ensure a supply of water, whether from lakes, rivers, springs, or irrigation canals. Sometimes the monopolization of water was even greater than the monopolization of the land itself and was more important an instrument for dominating the countryside (Chevalier 1970: 223). There was no real usurpation of Indian lands by the Spaniards in the early years of the colonial period, while land was still of little value. As Gibson (1964: 272) points out, Spanish accumulation of land did not become important until the market had developed sufficiently to make it profitable for Spaniards, and particularly for officials, merchants and miners who had access to capital, to invest in land and in agricultural production. Spanish encroachment on Indian lands was most marked, of course, near the large concentrations of urban population. Thus, in the Valley of Mexico 'an enormous part, considerably more than half, of the agricultural and pastoral areas of the Valley was officially transferred from Indian to Spanish hands during the first century after the conquest. Furthermore, it was a universal tendency among Spaniards to encroach beyond the limits of the grants' (Gibson 1964: 277).

Elsewhere in the country, Spanish appropriation of Indian lands occurred to a lesser degree. According to Chevalier (1970: 82) before the middle or end of the seventeenth century only a small part of cultivated land, especially in the *tierra caliente* of the coasts, came into Spanish hands. Nonetheless the consequences for Indian agriculture were disastrous. Most of the Spanish accumulation of land was not through legal grant by the state but through individual acquisition through purchase, extortion, forced sale, or simple occupation. Legal approval, as in so many other developments during the Spanish colonial period, more often than not came later. The state, in exchange for its grant of approval, tried whenever possible to exact some price from the Spaniard who sought legal title to the land he already possessed (Gibson 1964: 406). Beginning in the 1570s and especially after the epidemic of 1576, Spanish *haciendas* arose in or spread to the so-called *tierras baldías* or vacant lands. After 1593 and in response to its own growing financial needs, the crown demanded payment for these lands from the Spaniards and others who sought them. At the same time and for the same reasons, the crown offered to legalize *hacienda* lands that had already been acquired extra-legally. The lands called *demasias*, or lands in excess of those acquired legally, were made subject to *composiciones* (legalization) if the *hacendado* paid the crown a certain sum of money. Thus vast areas of land that had been acquired extra-legally or illegally, and especially pasture lands that had not previously been subject to *hacienda* ownership, were granted legal title of ownership. Of course, by no means all of the assessments were ever paid by the Spaniards who nonetheless became legal owners (Chevalier 1970: 264–5). Some of the *demasias* were also sold to others. Thus in 1629 the crown ordered the sale of 650 *caballerías* of wheat and sugar lands in Cuaútla, Atlixco, Oaxaca, and Toluca, as well as some sheep-grazing lands near Querétaro (Chevalier 1970: 269).

Later in the colonial period, as they were also to do at the end of the nineteenth century, Spanish landowners 'denounced' Indian lands as being vacant, whether they were or not, in order to acquire them for themselves (Gibson 1964: 285–6). Thus many remaining Indian communities found themselves entirely surrounded and even overrun by Spanish latifundia. Since autonomous Indian communities were in law entitled to lands and were protected by the 500 and 1,000 *vara* limits against encroachment by Spaniards, the latter claimed that the community whose lands they wanted was not a legal community. Many Indian communities were thus left with nothing but the land on which their houses stood. Paradoxically, it was therefore in the interest of the Spaniards to claim that they and their ancestors had treated the Indians so harshly as to destroy their communities and it was in the latter's interest to claim that this had not been the case and that they had retained their freedom. For it was on the status of the community that the Indians' right to land turned (Gibson 1964: 285–99). Already in 1599, reports Mendizábal, 'armies of commissioners and scribes were sent to throw the Indian towns off the lands that were wanted by the Spanish or Criollo latifundism; and the inhabitants of the large centres of population who lacked the economic means of survival and opportunities for work began to flow over towards the depopulated *haciendas*' (Mendizábal 1945–6: ii, 495).

The question arises why the Indians gave up their land to the Spanish *latifundistas*. One reason, of course, was that at the turn of the seventeenth century many Indian settlements were partially or substantially depopulated, the Indian communities were weakened by population loss, and the Indians were no match economically or politically for the growing power of the Spanish landowners (Chevalier 1970: 216–17). Further, since land without an owner reverted to the crown, the Indian chiefs had an additional incentive to sell land to the Spaniards to avoid its loss when owners died (Chevalier 1970: 217). Yet even without this institutionally created incentive, Indians (and particularly Indian chiefs) were obliged to sell their lands due to the economic pressure of debts and political pressure or physical force exerted by the Spaniards harassed them until they sold out (Chevalier 1970: 213). That such pressure affected many Indians and even non-Indians is suggested by the fact that there were many sales of very small pieces of land: in 1619 and 1620 for example a *hacienda* near Mexico was formed, with the exception of one larger piece of land, out of purchases of land for 2, 4, 8, 11, and 14 pesos (Chevalier 1970: 215). Once the Indians sold their land it was lost to them for ever (Chevalier 1970: 217) though there may have been some Indian recuperation of land at the beginning of the nineteenth century (this is a deduction; I have not yet found any evidence). *Latifundista* appropriation of lands during this period was not limited to Indian lands; the lands of poor Spaniards and *mestizos* were by no means spared. All possible legal and illegal means were resorted to in the quest for land, irrespective of who its previous owner had been.

The accumulation of land by the latifundia went to the extent of amassing land which 'They neither sow nor plant, they do not build the mills or ranches for which they were given the land. . .and so it remains barren; and the labourers and others who would work it dare not. .' (quoted from a 1564 royal *cedula* by Chevalier 1952: 185). That is, in the words of an *oidor* speaking in 1585, 'Estancia founders have striven, either by grant or purchase, to corner all the surrounding sites; some stockmen own estancias for eight, ten, or twenty leagues beyond the one which they have stocked, and stocked inadequately. The other inhabitants are seriosly inconvenienced and misused; they cannot find a single site left, owing to the quantity of land occupied, or rather, usurped, in a manner contrary to all reason' (Chevalier 1970: 141). In other words, the *latifundistas* were monopolizing land beyond that which they could use for agricultural purposes.

Why did they do so then, and why have they done so since? The answer is given quite explicitly by Chevalier:

> The proprietors of the largest haciendas, while utilizing money advances and perpetual debts to procure needed labor, had other means at their disposal. One convenient procedure was to take the Indians' own land away from them, thus obliging the Indians to work for hire, or to become sharecroppers or farmers on the great estates, capable of supplying sufficient manpower in seasons of heavy field work.   (Chevalier 1970: 285)

In fact, as Chevalier suggests elsewhere (1970: 215), the best way to get *gañánes* and peons was to take the lands away from the Indian towns. The other source of workers as well as of land was other Spaniards. The *latifundistas* not only deprived smaller Spanish owners of their lands and thus converted them into labourers or tenants as well, but they also raided their neighbouring *latifundistas* for labour, Indian and Spanish, by offering one attraction or another, usually loans that would then tie the tenants to them (Chevalier 1970: 284). This method of obtaining labour, and cheap labour, is common to latifundia agriculture throughout. More significantly perhaps from the point of view of the regional or national economy as a whole, the pursuit of monopoly control over labour, other resources, and even over trade channels and sources of finance through the monopolization of the essential complementary resource, land, is one of the most important and common causes (though largely unobserved) for the growth and continuation of latifundium agriculture and its associated inefficiency of resource utilization (this from the social though not from the private monopoly point of view). (For more detailed analysis of this point, see Frank 1967: chapter 4 and Frank 1969: chapter 16.)

9 ❧ The organization of labour

The expansion of the *hacienda* and the growth of its monopoly over land were also accompanied by the development of a new labour institution. This was the introduction of agricultural workers variously called *gañánes*, or *laborios* or *naborios*, who were formally free workers but who were in practice tied to the *hacienda* by debt and/or tenancy ties. This institution increasingly replaced the previous institutions of the *encomienda* and *repartimiento*. Thus this innovation marked the passing of the conceptions held by the Spaniards during the first two periods of colonial rule when they had sought to maintain the Indian economy separate from the Spanish one, and it signified the development during the third period of Spanish rule of a single economy into which Spaniards, Indians and *mestizos* were all fully integrated, albeit with unequal benefits to themselves. The immediate impetus to the development of *gañán* labour as a dominant institution was the labour shortage created by the epidemic of 1576–8 – just as the epidemic of 1545–8 had been the immediate impetus to the development of the *repartimiento* institution. As Gibson suggests, 'The sequence of agricultural labor institutions – encomienda, repartimiento, private employment – may be understood as a progressive adjustment to a shrinking labor supply.' (Gibson 1964: 246).

As was noted previously, the supply of Indian labour became increasingly short after the epidemic of 1576. Attesting both to this shortage and to the commercial penetration of the Mexican agricultural economy, Indian wages registered an important increase between 1575 and 1600 (Zavala 1943: 97). The minimum wage in *repartimiento* labour was three to four *reales* a week before 1594 and six *reales* a week after that (Chevalier 1970: 68). In 1608 free agricultural workers were getting 5 to 6 pesos a month in Nombre de Dios, and 50 to 60 pesos a year in Zacatecas at the beginning of the seventeenth century. At the same time Spaniards were still getting 300 to 400 pesos a year (Chevalier 1970: 279). As the shortage of labour increased, the Indians were able to demand and get higher wages and better working conditions (Borah and Cook 1962: 7).

Lacking *encomienda* or *repartimiento* labour, Spanish entrepreneurs began to hire free workers, at first for their *obrajes* or textile workshops, and to convert them into debt-tied peons. The employment of free workers then spread to mines and *haciendas* as well (Gibson 1964: 253–6). By 1580 owners of *haciendas* in the Valley of Mexico began to resort to private agricultural employment (Gibson 1964: 246). Before the end of the sixteenth century, *latifundistas* were doing so near Puebla as well (Chevalier 1970: 280). In the beginning, these landowners only hired a small number of agricultural workers (called *acasillados* because they lived on the farm for year-round work) and supplemented these with others for seasonal work (Gibson 1964: 253–4).

The private employment of formally free but actually tied labour became the dominant labour institution despite resistance to this development from *encomenderos*, receivers of *repartimiento*, and Indian towns and chiefs, whose control over the shrinking supply of labour was increasingly threatened and finally eliminated by this new development. The passage from slavery to *encomienda*, to *repartimientos*, to *gañán* labour – even if the freedom of the latter was that of a proletarian at best and of a serf at worst – no doubt represented some progress in human labour institutions. Nonetheless, like the abolition of slavery elsewhere, this development no doubt owed less to the magnanimity of those who benefitted from the labour institutions to be replaced, or even to the social consciousness of the 'society' or of those of its members who benefitted from the new labour institution, than it did to the productive changes and to the growing economic strength and political power of the new entrepreneurs, which permitted the latter to obtain laws and to create institutions that served their economic interests better than those of their relatively ever weaker rivals.

The *encomienda* had been weakened and the *encomenderos* suffered blow after blow almost from the beginning. Already in 1536, tribute payments to the *encomenderos* were officially fixed, even if the limits were perhaps not always observed in practice. By 1549 *encomenderos* had been prohibited from exacting tribute in the form of labour. At the same time, the succession laws were modified so as to limit the grant of an *encomienda* to the span of two lives or to one, with subsequent reversion to the crown, rather than the earlier nearly unlimited grant. After 1550, Gibson suggests, no new instances of Indian exploitation in the Valley of Mexico could be attributed to the *encomienda* (Gibson 1964: 80). Chevalier counts in 1560 480 *encomenderos* with a combined tribute of 377,734 pesos (Chevalier 1970: 118). By 1602, the number of *encomenderos* was down to 140 and their combined tribute fell to 300,000 very much devalued pesos. By that time, Gibson suggests, *encomendero* authority was all but gone and replaced by royal authority (Gibson 1964: 81). Indeed as we saw earlier, beginning with the shortages of the 1580s, the *encomenderos* had already been obliged to deliver their tribute grain to the viceregal or municipal authorities at the low market prices. In the words of Lee, 'All of these measures served to reduce the *encomenderos* to the status of private collectors of such taxes as the state permitted' (Lee 1947: 658). By the beginning of the seventeenth century the *encomiendas* represented a very small source of capital. Many mines, sugar plantations, *haciendas*, and commercial houses provided an income very much larger than the very best *encomiendas*, and the richest man in New Spain had for some time been a businessman without any *encomienda* at all (Chevalier 1970: 119).

The decline of the *repartimiento* as a labour institution followed the decline of the *encomienda* by one or two generations. A *cedula* of 1601 established that the *repartimiento* was to be abolished in agriculture, building, and everywhere else except mining; that the *jueces repartidores* who had allocated Indian labour to Spanish recipients were to be abolished, and that Indians were henceforth to sell their labour to any buyer. The edict does not seem to have taken effect immediately but rather gradually, and it was repeated in essentially the same terms in 1609. Important new edicts to the same effect were issued in 1627 and then again in 1632 and 1633. By this latter date, probably as a result of the competition of the rising institution of *gañán* labour rather than on account of the edicts against the declining institution of *repartimiento* labour, forced labour had finally been eliminated everywhere in New Spain except in some mines. By then, many members of Indian communities had chosen to settle on *haciendas* and to become *gañán* labourers, if only to escape from their obligations to the community and through it to receivers of *repartimiento* labour, since with the decline of the Indian population the burden on the remaining Indians had increased (Gibson 1964: 248, Borah 1951: 5). By the time of the flooding of the Valley of Mexico in 1632–3, employers who had ensured their supply of labour through the employment of *gañánes* were able to resist the crisis better than those who had to depend on *repartimiento* labour. Perhaps this is why the definitive order for the abolition of the *repartimiento* (except in mines) came at that time.

Silvio Zavala summarized the development of *gañán* labour thus:

For years past the Spanish farmers had begun to attract to their farms the Indian of the neighboring villages who were known as *gañánes* or *laboríos*. Thus, instead of waiting for the periodic assignments of Indians by the public authority, they had Indian families continuously in residence on their own lands as labourers...Moreover, the landowners had begun to do everything in their power to strengthen their hold on the *gañánes* by depriving them of freedom to leave their farm at will. The legal means of accomplishing this purpose was found in advances of money and goods, which bound the *gañán* to the land by placing him in debt. This method and not the old encomienda of the sixteenth century constitutes the true precursor of the Mexican hacienda of more recent times. Under the latter system the master is the owner of the land through grant, purchase or other legal title or perhaps only as a squatter and he attracts the *gañánes* to his lands and then keeps them there by means of debts. Liberal thought in the period of colonization did not fail to look with mistrust upon this system of agrarian servitude through debt, and it denounced the system as formerly it had denounced slavery, the *encomienda*, and *cuatequil* [*repartimiento*]. The Spanish government made significant provisions for limiting the amount of legal indebtedness...In spite of these restrictions...the farmers had succeeded in extending the system of *gañanes* and had secured it by means of debt...the growing number of peons and the isolation of the estates gave rise gradually to the custom of punishment of the peons by the master or his representatives; but this does not mean that the latter possessed judicial authority, for the king's justice intervened whenever a serious crime was committed. The system of peonage thus has colonial roots, but in that period the vigilance of public authorities afforded a measure of protection to the laborers. When, subsequently, laissez faire and other abstinence theories of public law left the peons alone and defenseless against the economic power of their masters, the harshness of the *hacienda* regime increased and the population and importance of the Indian villages steadily diminished in comparison with the estates employing peons.   (Zavala 1954: 98–100)

The change in the quality of the *hacienda* regime probably came about less through changes in ideology than for economic reasons. As Borah suggests; 'the development of profitable urban and foreign markets for foodstuffs and special crops in the nineteenth century made possible a much sharper exploitation aimed at large commercial profit' (Borah 1966: 24).

In 1642 Viceroy Palafo y Mendoza prohibited those in debt to their *hacienda* employer from leaving the *hacienda*. This would seem to confirm the common belief that the contraction of debt had become an important instrument whereby landowners and other employers assured themselves of a cheap supply of workers over whom they exercised considerable force. Nonetheless, many Indians had begun to settle on Spanish *haciendas* and were allowed a small plot of ground which they farmed for themselves, in exchange for the labour they gave the landowner when he needed it. According to Chevalier (1970: 287), this kind of tenancy was more important than debt peonage in assuring the landowner the supply of labour he needed. According to Gibson (1964: 255), in the Valley of Mexico less than half of the *hacienda* workers were subject to debt peonage at the end of the colonial period. Gibson argues furthermore that the quantity of debt owed was not really very large. Indeed, he suggests that rather than being a mark of the *hacendado's* power over his peon the amount of debt owed by workers was a measure of the workers' bargaining power in getting loans from the landowners. This bargaining power increased when the shortage of labour became more acute; and it manifested itself in the payment of existing debt and the extension of further loans to workers by one landowner who thereby attracted workers from other landowners (Gibson 1964: 253–6). Thus, Gibson argues, the *hacienda* and debt peonage in particular were less coercive in the seventeenth century than other labour institutions had been previously (Gibson 1964: 249, 256). Observing that the size of the natural family had increased again, Borah suggests that debt peonage life on the *hacienda* probably represented an improvement for most Indians at that time (Borah 1951: 432). As we saw above, both Borah and Zavala suggest that working conditions on the *hacienda* became much more severe in the nineteenth century. This evaluation of the welfare of the peasants is consistent with the thesis of agricultural depression; for it may be observed that in general commercially bad times for the *hacienda* permitted a higher level of subsistence for tenants, while demand-generated expansion of *hacienda* agriculture led it to deprive tenants of more of their land and labour. This was not the case, however, for agricultural labourers who had no plots of ground on the *hacienda* for their own farming. They were dependent upon wages and could demand higher wages when the demand for their labour increased. But I have argued that in important parts of New Spain there was no agricultural depression at this time and that, on the contrary, the *hacienda* was expanding. This suggests that the tenants were not improving their conditions and that, if they did register any improvement, it was not because they had gained in their subsistence production through their transfer from the Indian communities to the hacienda. Rather it was because they had increased their ability to escape from labour obligations outside of agriculture (and these were declining anyway except for the labour draft in the Valley of Mexico for the construction of the water works). If the peasants were even further deprived of their livelihood in the nineteenth century, this only shows that commercial pressure then was greater than it had been during the first half of the seventeenth century, not that it was absent during the latter period. This pressure probably, did decline around the middle of the seventeenth century, before increasing again later, especially at the end of the eighteenth century after the opening of 'free trade'.

10 ✦ Some characteristics of the *hacienda*

We may go on to examine some further characteristics of the *hacienda* and to consider the character of the institution that grew up in Mexico at the beginning of the seventeenth century and which, although often transformed, has survived to our day in many parts of Latin America. The most commonly accepted thesis about the character of the *hacienda* is that it began as a feudal institution and that it has remained one since. The thesis is summarized by one of its relatively few opponents, Jan Bazant:

> One of the authors of this thesis is Andres Molina Enriquez, who coined the phrase that the *hacienda* is not a business but a seigniory, the product of vanity and pride, within whose territorial limits the owner exercises the dominion of a feudal lord. The thesis of Molina Enriquez was later systematically developed in the works of McBryde, Tannenbaum and Simpson, who maintained that the *hacienda* was a unit which was essentially self-sufficient, autarkic, and independent of the market, and that production was developed on a small scale and in units of small operation, using small renters, sharecroppers, or peons; in other words, that the economy of the *hacienda* and more especially its mode of production were feudal in the sense of our definition. It is true that these writers were really referring to Porfirian times (1880–1910), but we can suppose that the *hacienda* did not change essentially in the course of its existence. (Bazant 1950: 88)

Bazant also notes the implications and significance of this thesis: 'If agriculture is typical of Mexico, the hacienda is typical of its agriculture. Therefore, if the hacienda is feudal, so is agriculture, and therefore so is Mexico taken as a whole. The thesis about the feudal character of the hacienda is, therefore, of great importance' (Bazant 1950: 88). The implications extend still farther beyond those noted by Bazant: if Porfirian Mexico was feudal, then the Mexican revolution of 1910 was an

78

anti-feudal revolution, at least in part. That is, in fact, the almost universally accepted interpretation of that revolution. Elsewhere in Latin America, no revolution of the Mexican type has occurred, and the feudal regime is said still to persist. The conclusions drawn are that a bourgeois, anti-feudal revolution has yet to take place.

Bazant's summary argument does reflect the general argument fairly accurately. Bazant's own rejection of the argument is based on his rejection of the premise that the *hacienda* itself was feudal. Yet the whole argument is invalid irrespective of the validity of this premise. As the above inquiry into the first hundred years of the history of Mexican agriculture suggests (and as the examination of its later history would make still more clear), the essential character of Mexican agriculture, still less that of Mexico as a whole, cannot be determined from the character of its most dominant labour institution, be that the *encomienda*, the *repartimiento*, the *hacienda*, or now the *ejido*. It was not the character of an institution, much less its changing characteristics, which determined the system as a whole (and this system extended far beyond Mexico to the ends of the earth reached by Mexican silver); rather the institution was itself determined by the structure and development of the system as a whole. We have seen above how this structure and development brought the *hacienda* into being. The *hacienda* was not an institution transplanted by feudal lords from feudal Europe. It came into being on Mexican soil, as elsewhere, in response to local conditions and local needs, although these in turn may have been influenced or even determined by changing conditions and needs in Western Europe or in the world mercantile capitalist system taken as a whole.

Nonetheless, it is of some interest to take note of the *hacienda*'s characteristics and character. Of particular interest is the derivation of the institution's name, *hacienda*. Chevalier himself points out the history of the word and the significance of its history for an appreciation of the institution:

Not until then [the seventeenth century] did the word *hacienda* take on its modern meaning. At the beginning, it had designated liquid assets, and was used for any sort of real or movable property. People talked of 'migrating sheep haciendas' – flocks with their shepherds –...The word was even extended to cover 'mining haciendas' alongside 'harvest and livestock haciendas'. All these acceptations were current in the seventeenth century...In 1637, Mexico City's municipal government [wrote]: 'There are in this realm only six types of...[*haciendas*], namely, housing, farm lands, flour mills, sugar refineries, and cattle and sheep raising.'   (Chevalier 1970: 264, 231)

We might add that even today the ministry of the treasury in various countries of Latin America is called the 'ministry of *hacienda*'. The word *hacienda*, then, did not come to be applied to an agricultural property and institution or specifically to designate that institution until entrepreneurs came to invest their capital in this landed institution, until they amalgamated their investments in mining, commerce, and land into one single enterprise, until finally they concentrated their investment in the agricultural rather than in the mining or some other *hacienda*. Thus, Chevalier observes, 'The word *hacienda*, unlike *estancia*, suggests capital invested in land, capital that the *ricos homes* had spent to dam streams, build permanent installations, and buy slaves, animals, and a complete stock of iron implements and wagons' (Chevalier 1970: 167). That the latifundium came predominantly to be called a *hacienda* (where it was not called a plantation) is not, then, the result of a fictitious implantation of Spanish feudal institutions in Mexico and Latin America, but can be explained by function in the historical process of the mercantile capitalist system.

Another characteristic of the *hacienda* may be said to be the kind of men who owned them. 'The great *hacendados* were financial entrepreneurs', we are told by Gibson (1964: 292). It was they who founded the *complejo real minero hacienda*. We observed above how mine owners acquired lands and incorporated them into a vast commercial enterprise. Furthermore, as Chevalier notes, 'Many merchants became landed proprietors, for real estate was a safe investment in their eyes' (Chevalier 1970: 144). Chevalier observes elsewhere:

Arizmendi Gogorrón appears in some respects a modern industrialist and businessman. He founded a number of important mining and mixed haciendas, went into partnership with one Acevedo to do some prospecting, and acquired an interest in many mines which he then developed. He also bought land in the Bajío, where he already owned ten estancias...; he wished to install irrigation on the new land.   (Chevalier 1970: 175–6)

Some of these entrepreneurs lived in Mexico City, 800 kilometers away from their lands (Chevalier 1970: 182). Others even moved to Spain to live off their earnings. Their agricultural enterprises, in the words of Borah were 'haciendas that were both units of production and means of stable investment in an age that had few other outlets for capital' (Borah 1966: 24).

The commercial reasons for the venture into the *hacienda* and the commercial character of the *hacienda* itself while business was good are evident from our earlier examination of the growth of the latifundium in Mexico. This commercial character had also been emphasized by Bazant:

> In considering the mercantile factor of wheat cultivation, we can say that very little was consumed on the *hacienda*, since the peons did not eat bread and the *hacendados* ate more *tortillas* [corn bread] than the Spanish inhabitants of the cities. Therefore, we can say that, apart from what was consumed on the *hacienda*, wheat was produced almost exclusively for the market [At the end of the eighteenth century] the markets were not to be discounted: the consumption per white inhabitant of the cities was the same as the consumption per inhabitant of Paris according to a calculation by Humboldt. Part of the total production was also exported...[W]ith respect to the mercantile character of maize production, the following may be said: apart from the market that still exist today, that is cities of comparable size to the European ones of that time, and apart from the trade between those regions with good harvests and those with bad, enormous quantities of maize were consumed by the beasts of burden, the most important means of transportation, and draft animals, that is, the most important source of energy in the mines and industries...[It] may be seen that maize was a commodity that was desired not only for direct consumption, but also as a source of energy in the capitalist production of goods. The mercantile character of maize then is evident.
>
> (Bazant 1950: 90, 93)

The *hacienda* was not merely commercial in that it produced commercial crops for the market or hired labour on the market. In the words of Eric Wolf, the *hacienda* was 'geared to sell products in a market', however successful or unsuccessful it may have been in doing so, given the ups and downs of the market. Gibson is still more explicit:

> A series of remarkable letters written between 1775 and 1785 by the administrator of the Hacienda de Molino de Flores near Texcoco to the hacienda owner in Mexico City describes more fully than any other known documents the daily life and economy of the late colonial hacienda. The letters effectively demonstrate that the hacienda was not maintained simply as a luxury estate for prestige in landholding, or in gentlemanly disregard of profit and loss. Molino de Flores concentrated on wheat, maize, and barley. The administrator

recorded his daily preoccupation with weather, prices, Indian labor, and the detailed schedule of agricultural production. His constant concern was whether to sell his produce at existing prices or to hold it in expectation of higher profits in the future, and he and the hacendado sometimes argued over the decision to sell immediately or later. Maize and wheat supplies suffered weekly depletion in the payments of rations to workers, a drain necessarily calculated in the estimates of future supplies and the decisions for retention or sale. Grain sometimes had to be sold in order to pay the wages of the peones. The administrator kept close watch over neighboring haciendas, observing when and what they planted, how they were affected by frosts and droughts, and what their crop yields were, for all this determined his competitive success or failure.   (Gibson 1964: 331)

We see then that the *hacienda was* operated for profit.

Moreover, much of the profit was derived from speculation in the market. After the exceptionally severe frosts of 27 and 28 August 1785, Gibson reports:

By October, in anticipation of the shortages to come, hacendados had closed their granaries and stopped selling. This artificially intensified the natural crisis, and consumers with money in hand were unable to buy. The price rose to four pesos per fangega in September and October, to four and one-half and five pesos in November, and to six pesos in the early weeks of 1786.
(Gibson 1964: 316)

Every period of natural disaster for which we have a record shows that the *latifundistas* exhibited the same kind of speculative behaviour. Only when popular uprisings against the shortages, as in 1692, threatened the physical safety of the landowners, merchants, and authorities and even the maintenance of the system itself, only then did the *hacendados* and merchants accede to official pressure to release stocked foodstuffs from their storehouses for immediate consumption (Gibson 1964: 327).

Hacendados in colonial times, no less than today, adjusted both their agricultural output and payment of their agricultural workers to fluctuations in the market:

Hacendados in the central portions of the Valley characteristically depended on the production of wheat and adjusted lesser sowings of maize to the relative or expected prices. Late colonial hacendados also capitalized heavily on the pulque market, competing directly and successfully with Indian private and community production. In the Zumpango area in the eighteenth century pulque production increased while sheep-herding decreased.
(Gibson 1964: 329)

Indians producing on a small scale, no less than Spanish *latifundistas* producing on a large scale, also responded to changes in market price and profitability:

The shifting emphasis from maize to maguey cultivation in the late sixteenth century may be documented in particular towns, such as Coatitlan...Men, women and children in Coatitlan carried on a pulque commerce, and Indian maize plantings were abandoned for the more lucrative trade...[The Coatitlan region was one] where the Indians' extensive plantings of maguey resulted not from aridity or impoverishment of soils but from the high profits to be derived from pulque sales   (Gibson 1964: 318–19).

When it came to making paments, the *hacendados* of the colonial period, like the Indians in the 1530s (see chapter 2 above) and all landowners everywhere since then, sought to pay in whatever way would cost them least: 'They could offset the effects of variation in price by paying laborers in money when the price of maize was high or alternatively in maize when the price was low – a practice that transferred the burden of price fluctuation to the Indian workers' (Gibson 1964: 326).

Being geared to the market, the *hacienda* was geared not only to increases in market demand but also to declines.

A glut quickly lowered prices to the point where commercial agriculture met its ruin. Thus the hacienda played safe by always producing below capacity. It never staked all or even most of its land on the vagaries of the market. In times of uncertainty, it could always fall back on its own resources and feed itself. It possessed its own defences, which it never jeopardized...To produce the cash crop, a hacienda would farm only a small portion of its total land resources – its best land.   (Wolf 1959: 205)

Strange then is the judgement of Chevalier that 'The landed proprietor's peculiar mentality was not conducive to thinking in terms of efficient production. He acquired land, not to increase his earnings, but to eliminate rivals and hold sway over an entire region' (Chevalier 1970: 311). Yet Chevalier himself has shown how, in colonial times in Mexico no less than elsewhere in Latin America even today, the accumulation of land and other resources far beyond the quantity used in actual production and the consequent idling of significant parts of the owners' and the economy's resources were the necessary means and products of the pursuit of maximum profit. The maximization of profit necessitated the continuous attempt to get

monopoly control of a significant sector of the highly monopolistic capitalist market. (Perhaps one of the clearest cases of
this phenomenon is the European monopolization of land in
central and southern Africa in order to oblige the Africans to
sell themselves into wage labour at subsistence and less than
subsistence wages. See Woddis 1960: chapter 1.) All of the
fundamental characteristics of the *hacienda*, including its mode
of production and labour relations which are so generally
attributed to the survival of feudal institutions or feudal
mentality, can, with much greater faithfulness to reality, be
derived from the structure and development of the monopolistic mercantile, industrial, and financial capitalist system.
This capitalist system is riddled with contradictions of which we
may cite one example:

the 'good' times of Indian agriculture might be times of hardship for the
haciendas, for the well-filled hacienda granary was most effective under the
prospect of rising prices. On the other hand, the critical years for Indian
agriculture were periods of relative prosperity for the haciendas, which
extended their controls from Spanish markets to Indian markets, notably in
maize and pulque, displacing Indian supplies and continuously reducing
Indian agriculture   (Gibson 1964: 334)

We may therefore agree with Bazant when he writes:

In summary I subscribe integrally to the words of Marco Antonio Duran
whom I quote herewith: 'By 1910 Mexican agricultural organization was
capitalist organization. Of course it did not produce on the basis of serfs but
of wage labor. It was not composed of closed economies. There was
production of goods and mercantilism existed, characteristics that cannot
co-exist with feudalism.   (Bazant 1950: 94)

References

Aguilar Monteverde, Alonso. 1968. *Dialéctica de la economía mexicana*. Mexico, Editorial Nuestro Tiempo

Arcila Farías, Eduardo. 1950. *Comercio entre Venezuela y México en los siglos XVII y XVIII*. Mexico, El Colegio de México

1955. *El siglo ilustrado en América. Reformas económicas del siglo XVIII en Nueva España*. Caracas, Ediciones del Ministerio de Educación

1957. *El régimen de la encomienda en Venezuela*. Seville, Escuela de Estudios Hispano-Americanos

Bagú, Sergio. 1949. *Economía de la sociedad colonial. Ensayo de la historia comparada de América Latina*. Buenos Aires, El Ateneo

Baraona, Rafael *et al.* 1960. *Valle del Putaendo: Estudio de estructura agraria*. Santiago, Instituto de Geografía de la Universidad de Chile

Bazant, Jan. 1950. 'Feudalismo y capitalismo en la historia de México', *El Trimestre Económico*, Mexico, XVII: 65 (January–March)

Borah, Woodrow. 1951. 'New Spain's century of depression', *Ibero-Americana*, Berkeley, XXXV

1966. 'Colonial institutions and contemporary Latin America: political and economic life' in Lewis Hanke (ed.), *Readings in Latin American History*, II, 18–25. New York, Thomas Crowell Co.

Borah, Woodrow and Cook, S. F. 1962. 'La despoblación de México Central en el siglo XVI', *Historia Mexicana*, XII (July–September)

Borde, Jean and Góngora, Mario. 1956. *Evolución de la propriedad rural en el Valle de Puange*. Santiago, Instituto de Geografía de la Universidad de Chile

Brading, David A. 1971. *Miners and Merchants in Bourbon Mexico, 1763–1810*. Cambridge, Cambridge University Press

Chaunu, Pierre. 1956. 'Comentario' in François Chevalier, 'La formación de los grandes latifundios en México', *Problemas Agrícolas e Industriales de México* (January–March)

Chevalier, François. 1952. *La formation des grands domaines au Mexique*. Paris, Institut d'Ethnologie

1956. 'La formación de los grandes latifundios en México', *Problemas Agrícolas e Industriales de México* (January–March). Spanish edition of Chevalier 1952

1970. *Land and Society in Colonial Mexico: The Great Hacienda*. Berkeley and Los Angeles, University of California Press. English edition of Chevalier 1952

Cline, Howard F. 1949. 'Civil congregations of the Indians in New Spain 1598–1606', *Hispanic American Historical Review*, XXIX

Cockcroft, James D. 1968. *Intellectual Precursors of the Mexican Revolution 1900–1913*. Austin, University of Texas Press

Cook, Sherburne F. and Borah, Woodrow, 1960. 'The Indian population of Central Mexico, 1531–1610', *Ibero-Americana*, Berkeley, XLIV

Cook, Sherburne F. and Simpson, L. B. 1948. 'The population of Central Mexico in the sixteenth century', *Ibero-Americana*, Berkely, XXXI

Costeloe, Michael P. 1967. *Church Wealth in Mexico*. Cambridge, Cambridge University Press

Florescano, Enrique. 1965a. 'El Abasto y la legislación de granos en el siglo XVI', *Historia Mexicana*, XIV (April–June)

   1965b. 'Agricultura e industria en Veracruz a fines del Virreinato', *Historia y Sociedad*, Mexico, II

Frank, Andre Gunder. 1967. *Capitalism and Underdevelopment in Latin America*. New York, Monthly Review Press. Revised and enlarged 1969. English edition. Harmondsworth, Penguin Books 1971

   1969. *Latin America: Underdevelopment or Revolution*. New York, Monthly Review Press

   1972. *Lumpenbourgeoisie: Lumpendevelopment*. New York, Monthly Review Press

Furtado, Celso. 1965. *Economic Growth of Brazil*. Berkeley, University of California Press

Gibson, Charles. 1964. *The Aztecs under Spanish Rule*. Stanford, Standford University Press

Góngora, Mario. 1960. *Origen de los 'inquilinos' de Chile Central*. Santiago, Editorial Universitaria

González Casanova, Pablo. 1965. *La democracia en México*. Mexico, ERA English edition *Democracy in Mexico*. London, Oxford University Press 1972

Humboldt, Alexander von. 1966. *Political Essay on the Kingdom of New Spain*. 4 vols. New York, AMS Press Inc.

Larraz López, José. 1943. *La época del mercantilismo en Castilla 1500–1700*. Madrid, Atlas

Lattimore, Owen. 1962. *Inner Asian Frontiers of China*. Boston, Beacon Press

Lee, Raymond L. 1947. 'Grain legislation in colonial Mexico, 1575–1585', *Hispanic American Historical Review*, XXVII

López Gallo, Manuel. 1965. *Economía y política en la historia de México*. Mexico, Ediciones Solidaridad

López Rosado, Diego. 1968–71. *Historia y pensamiento económico de México*. Mexico, Universidad Nacional Autónoma de México

Marx, Karl. [1851–3]. *On Colonialism*. Moscow, Foreign Languages Publishing House

Matesánz, José Antonio. 1965. 'Introducción de la ganadería en Nueva España, 1521–1535', *Historia Mexicana*, XIV (April–June)

Mendizábal, Miguel Othón de. 1945–6. *Obras completas*. 6 vols. Mexico, Ed. Talleres Gráficos de la Nación

Millon, Robert. 1969. *Zapata: The Ideology of a Peasant Revolutionary*. New York, International Publishers

Miranda, José. 1952. *El tributo indígena en la Nueva España durante el siglo XVI.* Mexico, El Colegio de México

1965. *La función económica del encomendero en los orígenes del régimen colonial (Nueva España 1525–1531).* Mexico, Universidad Nacional Autónoma de México

Moreno Toscano, Alejandra. 1965. 'Tres problemas in la geografía del maíz, 1600–1624', *Historia Mexicana*, XIV

Ots Capdequí, José M. 1946. *El régimen de la tierra en la América española durante el período colonial.* Ciudad Trujillo, Editora Montalvo

Prado Junior, Caio. 1962. *Historia económica del Brasil.* Buenos Aires, Editora Futuro

Sandoval, Fernando. 1951. *La industria del azúcar en Nueva España.* Mexico, Universidad Nacional Autónoma de México

Semo, Enrique. 1972. *Historia del capitalismo en México.* Mexico, ERA

Sepúlveda, Sergio. 1959. *El trigo chileno en el mercado mundial.* Santiago, Editorial Universitaria

Simonsen, Roberto C. 1962. *Historia económica do Brasil (1500–1821).* 4th edn. Sao Paulo, Companhia Editora Nacional

Stein, Stanley and Barbara. 1970. *The Colonial Heritage of Latin America.* New York, Oxford University Press

Vitale, Luis. 1968. 'Latin America: feudal or capitalist?' in James Petras and Maurice Zeitlin (eds.), *Latin America: Reform or Revolution?* Greenwich, Fawcett Books

1968–72. *Interpretación Marxista de la historia de Chile.* 3 vols. Santiago, PLA

Wolf, Eric R. 1959. *Sons of the Shaking Earth.* Chicago, University of Chicago Press

Womack Junior, John. n.d. *Zapata and the Mexican Revolution.* Harmondsworth, Penguin Books

Woodis, Jack. 1960. *Africa: The Roots of Revolt.* New York, Citadel Press

Zavala, Silvio. 1943. *New Viewpoints on the Spanish Colonization of America.* Philadelphia, University of Pennsylvania Press

Zorita, Alonso de. 1965. *The Lords of New Spain: The Brief and Summary Relation of the Lords of New Spain.* London, Phoenix House

Index